CONTEMPORARY
WORLD ENGLISH POETS

Chief Editor
Dr. Ratan Ghosh

Executive Editors
Krishnasankar Acharjee
Binay Laha

Clever Fox
PUBLISHING

Chennai • Bangalore

CLEVER FOX PUBLISHING
Chennai, India

Published by CLEVER FOX PUBLISHING 2020
Copyright © Dr. Ratan Ghosh 2021
All Rights Reserved.

ISBN: 9789390850488

CONTEMPORARY WORLD ENGLISH POETS

PASCHIM BANGA ENGLISH ACADEMY, ESTD- 2019

Working for the promotion of Literature, Culture and Translation

Dr. Ratan Ghosh, The State President, *Paschim Banga English Academy*

Krishnasankar Acharjee, The State Vice- President, *Paschim Banga English Academy*

Binay Laha, The State General Secretary, *Paschim Banga English Academy*

FOREWORD

Contemporary World English Poets, an International Anthology of poems, is a unique and noble initiative from the part of a renowned Literary Society entitled **Paschim Banga English Academy** established in 2019 with a motive of promotion of Literature, Culture and Translation studies in general. The society is known for its selfless services for the inter-cultural exchanges across the globe and for its initiatives to unite all the poets and authors of the world under an umbrella. In spite of being its primary intention to work first for the Indian Nation it can't be denied that it goes beyond that. The society does not know any boundary of caste, Creed, culture, race, colour, religion and border. India, as a nation, has a rich cultural heritage and is known for universal brotherhood and peace. It is a nation that defines all daughters as the symbol of key power and worships all mothers as 'Devi' or Goddesses. It can't be denied that even in the post-modern era women are treated as objects instead of human beings across the globe and they are marginalized, exploited and abused in different stages of their life. We, the Indians believe in the values of 'Maa' (Mother) cherished for long in the Vedic era. The cultural values, respect and dignity for daughters, mothers and to the elders are praiseworthy even today. That is why the society has confined its theme for the book on 'Gender, marginalization and Women trafficking'. The society will be working tirelessly following the principles of peace, love, brotherhood and unity and in doing so the society wishes to publish Translated, Transliterated and Edited books on Literature every year. I am overwhelmed seeing the list of the contributors from all over the world and the quality of the sublime verses. The initiatives as taken by the Editors, Dr. Ratan Ghosh, Krishnasankar Acharjee and Binay Laha are praiseworthy. I express heartfelt gratitude to all the renowned contributors who have enriched the quality of this book. I also thank to the Editors, to the other members and above all to the publisher for bringing out such a nice Anthology.

Dr. Parthapratim Dasgupta
Novelist and Academician,
The Principal, Barasat College, Kolkata

PREFACE

Contemporary World English Poets, an International Anthology of Poems and Paintings, is an initiative from Paschim Banga English Academy compiled and edited by Dr. Ratan Ghosh, Krishnasankar Acharjee and Binay Laha. The Anthology features around seventy renowned poets and their powerful poems from all over the world. The book defines the issues like Children and Women abuse, Women Trafficking, Gender Biases, Voices of the Third Gender or Transgender and the Voices of the Marginalized in the context of the present day. It can't be denied that woman is treated as secondary being even today. The issues like hegemony, marginalization, Feminism and any other isms especially in case of Gender Study are only showcased in the pages of the book shelves for the intellectual debates. But the ground reality if observed closely appears to be same as it was in the last few decades. Women and weaker people are always kept in the margin and their voices never find any space in the society. They have to follow either the so-called patriarchal social structure or to copy what they are directed by their male counter-part. The present book tries to feature the voices and views of the women poets and the voices and views of those others who have a sensitive heart for the caged and the marginalized. Poetry though a sublime art can be a significant medium for the voices of the marginalized. In this book the readers can enjoy mostly the views of the renowned women poets who have made their own identity through the words of their verses.

Dr. Ratan Ghosh

CONTENTS

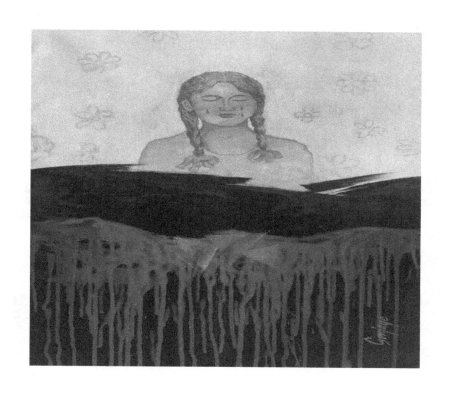

Copyright

Sonjaye Mauya, Mumbai

Copyright

Sonjaye Mauya, Mumbai

Copyright

Sonjaye Mauya, Mumbai

Lucilla Trapazzo, Rome, Italy

Psalmody (for a child bride)

Rock-a-bye baby my cinnamon girl;
It tinkles in silver your smile of milk.
Swing, my little on the seesaw
And gather the infinite plan of the game.

The hour thickens it stretches its hand. The name
crumbles. The rope breaks. You are the queen bride.
You are a child bride, my little green almond covered
with gold. Painful the violin - it screeches
it harvests the silence.

Wake up, wind bending the reeds, and unchain a storm
of sand and of ice. Grab her, wind filling the spikes
let her not feel, let it be light. Dissolve her, wind
Spreading the seeds, take her off flying in sunny fields
of wheat that is golden of stars and of flakes.

Open the doors tear up my womb; red is the night
and crushed, amphisbaena. Open the doors and pour in
the honey. Her name is written with colors and spices.
Open the doors and offer her dolls.

Open the doors tear up my belly.
Open the doors. Open the doors.

Burrnesha or the last Sworn Virgin

One gesture and it falls on the floor your skirt
final vestige of womanhood. A defiant braid surrenders
at your feet, with proud copper reflections. Your breast
is unripe. You touch your pomegranate skin
and bind it up.
Two cruel bandages are constraining the breath. Folded
is the bridal veil that once was your mother's
(A dream of apple and cinnamon guarded by camphor)
A fragment of glass reflects your trembling lips. On the bed
ragged pants are waiting for your milky skin.
Far away there's a chorus of voices and laments.
Your father
is resting in the largest room. Barely an amaranth scarf
hides the blossom of blood, memento of wild hunting.
You're alone now to keep the honor of home,
family and county.
Tomorrow, facing the elderly, with eyes of ice you'll deny
being a woman. It's a fight, a trade for your freedom.
Smoky cellars of *raki* and sweat are waiting for you.
Your belly
is barren forever. The law of mountains
and valleys, of impetuous
hastening rivers is written in blood since remote times
-*Alone, a Virgin is worth only six oxen* - Tomorrow,
you'll be a man.

For the love one hand, your sighs and your sorrow,
alone in the night
(In rural Albania, since the Middle Age, single women had
no honor, their possessions were disposed of and they were
not protected against violence. Only one solution remained
for them: to swear to remain virgins forever. The "sworn
virgins" became the Patriarchs of their families, with all
the burdens and honors of male authority. Today there is
about 40 sworn virgins in Albania)

Joanna Svensson, Swiden

MY HEART'S IRRESISTABLE LUST

In my solitude
When crumbs of time
Have fallen off the table
When others needs
And others doings
Have been fulfilling
Fulfilled…
There in my solitude
I gently gather them
All my undreamed dreams

I've always dreamed of dreaming
In order to realize
My heart's irresistible lust
My heart's deepest vocation

LIKE JEANNE D'ARC

Like Jeanne d'Arc
With a burning torch
With awesome powers
And a will to live
I have risen straight out of
The darkest swamp of falseness
A swamp that tried
To pull me down
And all of those
who's basked themselves
In my fame and in my glory
All who went
Behind my back
Slowly sink in their own muck
Yes, everyone
Who tried to ride me
And steal my own happiness' light
Gets it all in return
By a registered-letter post!

Jana Orlová (1986), Czech

My man and my guinea pig

On a walk in the morning
my boyfriend smiles gently
yes, he loves me so much.
How intriguing! A sudden thought:
maybe a man is even better
than a guinea pig
I used to cuddle when I was eleven

Ode to myself

Soft skin, dreamy thoughts
smell like cinnamon
Tender in the milky shirt
walking down the street
So nice to touch you
my women, my men

Alicia Minjarez Ramirez, Mexico

FOGGY SOLITUDES

I find myself close - distant
to the zephyr breeze, I question in vain.
Foggy solitudes, dressed up
As equinoxes in perennial springs.

I require to silence flooding words,
To silence tears adorning my face.
Sadness dwelling like a stowaway
In soul's murky mirrors.

Absence afflictions gradually succumb
between my barren hands.
Pointless to grasp into hope!
Reason outshines the fragmented heart
and the bare silence suffocates the stars.

Stars that won't shine upon nostalgia seas
taking away opacities and a shattered mirror
where my reflection fades away
Right now

Cracking in my own roots...
Dark memories, empty stealth,
And leaves scattered on the ground.

ABSENCE

You left
like rain…
After destroying
the bare countryside

Below the leaves
Your name
Flying with the wind
Foreseen the verse,
Its useless tessitura
Upon the unpropitious
Yesterday.
I still don't understand
the seven letters
Building
your absence.
It's not dark yet…
And the language
Of the sun
Is no longer the same.

Kapardeli Eftichia, Greece-Patra

Wounded Innocence

The Simple Truth in Small
dusty wear arches
bouquets of lilies silently
with white light
dye hair

The heart is pierced by your coming
fingers hit your chest awkwardly
and I'm scared of your childhood

Magical images of desperate beauty
They get lost in the arches
with vain hopes of destiny

I forget who I am
But it is not dark yet
I'm laying my hands
Relentless fire rays
they fill the arches of the wilderness

THE SILENCE OF VIOLENCE

A daily torment
Rape, humiliation,
Beating
There is no cry, only silence
In domestic violence
In poverty and misery

Ignored and despised
Abused
Without guilt and punishment
No protest
No hope

Behind the wall of silence
In rooms with closed windows
How many groans
And you desperate without joy
Who steals my dream who steals my joy bitter, rage?
I alone endure this violence silently
Lips, body innocence sweet
lost in the hands of a murderer one day I will be missing

YEARS OF REAL ESTATE

YEARS FOREIGN

It bathes me with light
the invincible form of the moon
stones carved into unruly rivers
They sound strange
on the roofs all day
the birds are no longer quiet

Years of real estate, years of foreign
Unlit streets that suffocate
Hands that do not care,
eyes that carve the void
I always liked those flowers

that enveloped the hidden shadows of the people
in the colors of the deserted beach

I walk alone through the wilderness
And friends on an empty
house closed, its circle
destiny plan secretly

Years real estate years foreign
Without a fair share
Deep roots, last fruitage
and those children's stories
in the window of the mind
Eternally trapped
Years you are silent, Years you forget

Paula Louise Shene, U. S. A

POOR PEOPLE DREAMS

People of every color, creed, and culture cry
Out to the heavens for justice to be brought nigh
On the oppressed some brothers against brothers
Rectitude lay within the heart or ego on druthers

Purpose for survival for many makes choices leading
Even should harm through actions leave siblings pleading?
Only, my brother, I cry for relief from your killings
Pushed into slavery and used as grist for the millings
Leaving our culture crushed, gashed, and bloodied
Evening tide sorrow surrounds home emotions muddied

Damned for generations, cursed by evilness personified
Rising above only in choice and repentance to abide

Everlasting laying down sword and shield
Almighty God to whom only I yield
Mankind must learn lessons on own or
Strike and forever fall dead on the field.

THE UNDERBELLY TRAGEDY

Twenty-five or was it thirty? Only,
Heaven knows how long ago the lonely
Ending of this young child's life

Underwent the horrors of heroin's strife
Needed to perform her duties as sex toy
Done by John's sucking away a child's joy
Everyone in the underbelly night time
Rested on anonymity while her teachers' crime
Became their ignoring the marked countenance greeted
Evident yearly seen of sweet to depressed to defeated
Lust by others led her into an early grave to go back to
Love that welcomed her home for walking a path's hue
Yielding laws to protect, but unless aware, millions grope

Treading the same lonely paths of
horror daily without joy or hope
Rescue never in sight with treats of violence to their kind
Again and again, physically but most
outrageous harm to mind
Groaning for succor, praying for society
to awaken and to aware
Ending their plight of slavery given lip service but few care
YOU, who read to the end, please help,
end their pleas of nightmare.

(This is the story of one young girl put into service on the streets of one of the major cities at the age of seven and given an overdose to kill her at age thirteen deemed too old to service the perversions of her Johns. We mourn for her and for all those who still are in this living hell of carnage we as a society turn a deaf ear and a blind eye. We have laws to stop. Let's start using them instead of bowing to the depraved.)

Miljana Živanović, Swiss

*Citizen of the World /
Travel Plus*

Child

Will it help if you say?
We are sorry?
You're far from home,
Look for the harbor to rest. . .
Child, find your way home
Know that the bed is waiting for you with love,
Hands so soft…
Who wanted to caress you. . .
There are always arms outstretched,
Where there is peace and warmth,

The home always remains a safe haven.
Two pairs of hands to say hello,
Two voices rejoicing,
Will toast home on return,
Welcome dear child. . .
You didn't understand,
you didn't notice. . .
Could it have been different?
On a trip, just where!
And switch off, she is rather alone…
Miljana Živanović

Dawn of new day

At the dawn of a new day
My soul is hiding again,
The lonely heart of the ignorant in the dark. . .
Now I wonder how it used to be. . .
Along the shores of life
Does the sun illuminate the world?
Will darkness give way to dawn full of strength?
sad or with a smile?

Oh! how to forget the dawn
and my magic window glass ?!
And I thought:
I'm not awake yet, I don't have a watch
and the immense silence feeds only my loneliness
with bread crumbs and morning dew,
without warmth and without sighs. . .

A new dawn will come. . .
I don't worry,
the light always comes back. . .
Miljana Živanović

Ngozi Olivia Osuoha, Nigeria

VOICES OF THE MARGINALIZED

There are voices in the dark
Yearning and yawning to be heard,
They are hidden, stigmatized
And some truncated.

See, they die in trauma and with trauma
They are sick of trauma
Down, downcast, downtrodden in downtown
They look yonder and they wonder
Because they are marginalized

Hunger, poverty, segregation, discrimination
Hate, bitterness and greed against them,
No one ever cares to hear or save them.

Voices, chants, prayers, wishes and dreams
Visions, missions and assignments
They wander in chaos
And wonder in bias,
Life dawns darkness on them.

Look, hear them roar, listen, help them soar
They have wings like eagles
Let them live without shackles.

CHILD AND WOMEN ABUSE

Children are gifts, special gifts
They bear talents and dreams
Lineages hook and line along them
Posterity anchors on them.

We kill them by actions and inactions
Abusing lives and misusing gifts,
We keep them far from peace.

We bring war carefully
And crush them carelessly
Mess them up for pleasure
Ruining futures carelessly and carefully

Abuses, curses, and fates
Barricading hopes and love
Silencing peace and unity
Demarcating the world

Children see hell, before being sent to hell
Women taste hell before trekking to hell
The world just hurts.

But we can keep them safe
Develop and love them better,
Children and women are lovely

Great gifts from nature
Beautiful treasures to be cherished
Yet we harm them cruelly.
©®

THE NONAGENARIAN DEITY

The nonagenarian deity
Instrumentalist, folklorist
Instrument of folklore
Mike Ejeagha.

In tongues and gongs
Songs; sung and unsung
Climbing rungs to right wrongs;
Melting hills like wax.

The beautiful rainbow
That dazzles against shackles,
The handsome glow
That twinkles even with wrinkles.

Male, now pale
Tale even of gale
Voice of the ancestors
Flute of the kindred spirit
Tune, concordance, trumpet
Melody and harmony
Mike Ejeagha

The nonagenarian deity
Festival of folklores,
Spirit of the gods
The legacy, the heritage

Mike Ejeagha
Anchor of tales
Succour of tails
Ripples on marble
Legend of the seeker

The golden voice
The diamond nuance
Platinum echo,
Hero of the land
Warrior of the people
Mike Ejeagha

Eulogies and elegies
Solemn assembly of the gods
Gathering of the spirits
The archive, the archivist

Mike Ejeagha
Tales by moonlight
Realities by sunlight
Leisure by daylight
Pleasure by broad daylight,
A legend gentleman

At ninety and one
You fought and won,
A unique nonagenarian
A prolific Nigerian,
Mike Ejeagha;
Another wonder of the world

Eliza Segiet, Poland

Translated by Ula de B
Tatyana Fazlalizadeh To

Power of Wisdom

Neither Gender nor skin color
Can't be the igniters of aggression
Experiencing the world,
Without torment from anyone,
is a human right.
When being broken
Must through power of wisdom
fight the lack of understanding.

Defensive force
Doesn't come from the void
Because...
the body's color is but a hull.
Inside it live
Memories, plans,
Dignity...
which must not be taken away

Monica Maartens, South African

SHATTERED DREAMS

Innocence and purity, so naive
Evil and wickedness it cannot conceive
Darkness opens in depravity and deceit
Another little life destroyed in defeat

Perfect trust all broken and shattered
Tiny body all bruised and battered
Hope and love devoured by pain
Terror and horror pouring like rain

Shame and withdrawal takes control
there are no words that can console

tiny hearts all ripped apart
hiding from a new days start

Beautiful dreams forever destroyed
silent screams so secretly employed
disgust and anger roars in ears
doors and voices feed the fears

A little child so fragile and tender
Sacred days for every gender
Always to be safe and protected
Never, ever abused or neglected
Zararia Yul © Copyright

TOGETHER

Spirits love to soar wild and free
Painting visions the soul can see
Hearts beat faster within an embrace
Igniting flames of passion and grace
Feelings dance and play with emotions
Sweet sensation of delightful commotions
it takes no notice of sex or gender
Flowing through heart and soul so tender
Male or female is merely appearance
covering bones and muscles for adherence
Both have brains and both have names
both have dreams and both play games
both need love to feel complete
both have shames they'd like to delete
man and woman both must eat
have desires they'd like to meet
standing together makes them strong
lifting each other from things that are wrong
building each other to rise up high
working together with a happy sigh
Zararia Yul © Copyright

Jialing Hu, China

Delighted Dependence, Homed

Delightedly rescued with my family,
Your dedicated shelter, care I depended on,
Gratitude spelled out proudly in my purrs,
Have you ever received?

Energized with curiosity to explore my surroundings,
Maybe I was walled in isolation before,
To serve the soundness of my compatriots,
Or this is me, always in the present.

I've learnt to coordinate with my fraternities,
I've learnt to behave brave before the slaves,
I am not unaware,
I am not unsure.

I am homed now with delight,
My cure sealed in the cans
That smells like you and me,
Like us, is home.

Behind

How much I miss and wish you around,
Considerate I have to be, to work hard.
I wrote above on a bed, in a room
Neither of which was mine,
Except for the tears on my face

Left behind, I was in the countryside with my kindest
grandma,
Far away, you were working in especial roc city,
Back then, I did fail to know its name.
Who's to blame? What's to help?
A writing hand empowered me,
With a haven for detachment and distress

Unconditional love and trust,
Support a family a family,
Despite of time and space,
Where reunion becomes unnecessary,
When union is the new normal

Behind you, I've always been,
Would you have me alongside?

Sue Zhu (淑文), New Zealand

Wind Chimes

All afternoon, he gazes out of the window
At the birthday gift hanging under the eaves and given last
year by his mom
From the city that imprisons her for most of her life

Its presence, at this impoverished home,
Seems too extravagant to be in tune
Its musical sound arouses his great yearning
Quietly, he counts how many times the wind returns

He knows, it is a long journey
To climb over the mountain and see flowers
blooming at the other side

He starts to envy the wind chimes— a pretty
girl with a slender waist
Who can get there before him?

He even has a huge crush on it
Two of them, no matter what
Are heavenly made to resemble each other?

Unable to Breathe

He couldn't breathe
Under the powerful knees of law enforcement officer
A loud child voice called mum
At this dying moment, mum was in his dream

She couldn't breathe
When the axe was raised high above her head by herded
A strange chilling gleam fell through the familiar face
The blood-boiling relatives cheered under the family tree

It couldn't breathe
The little glass jar imprisoned it for life
In the Penang seafood market in Malaysia, a grouper's tail
fin stopped swinging
I dared not to see its helpless round eyes
Staggering forward in the dark abyss, they could hardly
breathe
Dug out expensive fossil fuels and gems by exhausting the
light in their body
With many a pair of pale lungs in exchange for cheap text-
books
They bet on a bright future of their offspring
Unable to escape from the sky polluted by fossil fuels, they
fled from ancestral territories
Breathing in more carbon dioxide with horror

They were even caught, skinned alive,
or eliminated by human beings
Who superstitiously believed that their skins, furs and nails
could cure diseases?
They just couldn't breathe
When seeing these individual lives are strangled because of
skin colour, religion, greed and hatred
This is an utter violation of God's warnings
I just can't breathe freely...

Terana Turan Rahimli, Azerbaijan

I am a woman

I am not a painter
But I know a lot of colors
Most of painters are unaware of them:
Color of love, color of longing, color of grief...

I am not a composer
But I am able to hear the sounds
Of which any composer can't hear:
Sound harmony of parting, joining and hope

I am not a gardener
But as I feel the scents of flowers,
I also can feel the scent of days and months

Fragrant garland of colorful feelings
Gives a charm to my life
I am not a painter,
I am not a composer,
I am not a gardener either…
I am a woman
Whom the God created
In a pleasant hour…
There is the light of love of God
In my eyes and in my heart…

Don't look like me, my daughter!

They resemble you to me, my daughter
Don't look like me, my daughter!
Look at my gray hairs
Don't look like me, my daughter!

I eat a grief the clock round
I undress sorrow and put on grief.
I warn you as much as early
Don't look like me, my daughter!

Hide patience inside of you
Hide your secrets inside of you
Hide your face from the sorrow
Don't look like me, my daughter!

Pay attention neither to creeping shadow
Nor try to be knocked at any time
Become flames, try to destroy darkness,
Don't look like me, my daughter!

All around me are devils,
They don't let me become myself.
Oh, my darling, try to find your own being
Don't look like me, my daughter!

Selma Kopic, Tuzla, Bosnia and Herzegovina.

YOU DON'T NEED A LOT

Do you know how small you are?
When you prove your greatness
to someone smaller than you?
Do you know how weak you are?
When you show your strength
over someone who is weaker than you?
Do you know how cowardly you are?
When you show your courage by overcoming those
Who are more powerless than you?
When you respond to a gentle word with a curse
When you respond to caressing with rudeness,
When you respond to the love given by ignoring it
What do you expect?

You'll get fear in view, humility and retreat,
a false image of power and strength.
You'll get everything, but don't expect respect.
You need so little to be great, and strong and brave!
A kind word and a gentle touch are never too much.

When you marry a man from the village

Wife, mother, regular inventory
Doesn't deserve no reward or a gift
When she dies: let her die without moaning.
When she starts saying something
let her swallow and not say
With beans and hot, toasted pie
let her humbly wait for her man at home
Let her not ask him where he was
did he work or drink with his buddies
for God has given it to him
and people don't forbid
to spend his days in this way
He didn't justify himself to anyone
not even his father
so he won't to her either
He'll go to court, a righteous God sees everything!
What about her?
Wide field for her if there is better
or let her be silent and wait for God's justice
from now on and forever

Tali Cohen Shabtai, Israel

Woman

Observable
in you…
upon acquaintance…

To uplift
your ancient countenance
in your beauty…

You must warn
those who knew(you)
and those who are gone

About the mystery
Of the custom wherein
besides the burden
of your doom

For in this case
of such a woman

Her life can only
be known
by her death.

A wife

For his deeds
the mother
got
the decree.

His errors
Like Mark's of her judgment
in my vow…
She bore the yoke
a wife's
burden…
She will scorn,
Forever…

She will vow
to the secret-
Opened…
in ambush,

that disappeared in the west.

Meenakshi Mohan, U. S. A

Why was she A Story Written in Your Script

You shaped, you gave words
to the forms you created,
she like play dough
became whims of your moods
the rainbow of your nights,
the lyrics of your cheap Bollywood songs.

She, in her worn-out clothes, went to houses
to clean and cook and earn wages for a living.
The money went in your pocket
to your gambles and drinks, in her mumbles when she
raised concerns, in return
she became victims of bidi stub marks and blue-black eyes,
mental and physical abuse.

She knew not who to complain. She had a family
of four children to raise.
Your sons, born of her womb, go to schools to grow
up to carry your name.
Her daughter, submissive, quiet followed
her mother's footsteps –
Mother and daughter a check from one man to another
Who made the rules?

Why she became a commodity to be used
in any form and any shape?
Why her life awaited your signature to survive?
On her death, she remained a story written in your script.
Why, why, why?
---"An epitaph to "she" who worked as a housemaid in
India, Several years later, I came to know that she died of
an unknown cause. This story is of many other women like
her who become victims of male misogynistic attitudes. "

A Cry In Vain

"Mamma"
A last, despair, heart-quenching sound, as the soul escaped
the helpless, strangled body,
yes, "Perry, my child" a mother from heaven felt the pain
of a helpless forty-six-year-old son,
the pain of a father of two young children.

Was that even my twenty-dollar? I had no time to think of
what crime—
They pulled me out of my van, handcuffed,
pushed me on ground
their booted legs on my back, an excruciating pain,
a large mass compressed my neck –I pleaded,
"I can't breathe!"

I writhed in anguish, "I can't breathe. "My limbs stoic,
my ears ringing,
my lungs hyper inflating, I was getting
enveloped by darkness.
And I cried, over and over again, "I can't breathe, " "I can't
breathe, " "I can't breathe!"
You were there, "Did you hear me?"
Or ignored –I Was Black!

Those crucial eight-minutes --
George Floyd, "Perry" for his mother and aunt

Made history, Ignited the flame –

Note: "Skin is a terrain, said Toyin Ojih Odutola, a Nigerian artist about black life. Then, why is there such a disparate for skin colors? Charles De Arman said that the image we have of how a man or woman should look is down from the culture in which we live. Blacks themselves have not created the black image; their image has been created by white society. Trevor Noah on June 1st, 2020, on The Daily Show said, "... while the country is still dealing with COVID 19 Black Americans are not only dealing with the virus but also racism at the same time.

George Floyd's death on Memorial Day has reignited the call for equality, not only in America but also worldwide. George Floyd's brutal death was a cruel reminder that Black people in this country continue to be "crippled by the manacle of segregation and the chain of discrimination, " as Martin Luther King stated in his speech, *I have a dream.*

A cry in vain is a desperate voice of a marginalized race in this country and a call for Equality for marginalized citizens all over the world.

Jyotirmaya Thakur, U. K

DUMPED

Goddess Durga immersed in a nearby pond
Floating with stray ribs of straw and dry leaves non-stop
A baby corpse wrapped emerged in dark blue
Sadly a girl infant nipped in the bud by crooks.
A baby with pale pink placenta could not bloom
Dumped without mercy without a cry in doom
Saddened the crowd in spiritual hues
Spoiled their spiritual fervour by a brute
White babe quavering and rippling with clay pots
Still fresh marigolds and hibiscus dying in shrouds
Biological mother denied her dignity of fate
Divine mother buried her by her earthly weight.
Witness of this failure of humanity on stake
A beggar stretched her hands to bury her in a grave

Swimming across amidst weeds and worms
She held the corpse for a while in her bosom firm.
The desolate heart hungry for love and care
Had more courage than the crowd could dare
Like the goddess of clay that was swept away
Demons rise to put a goddess of flesh away.

TRAPPED

Poverty at the mercy of prestige,
Victim of honourable vestige,
The blueprint of their story,
Is blurred in Devil's chest history

No philosophy can teach morality,
Where generations survive servility,
No imagery apt to describe,
Penetrates darkness with scribe

Diction fails to cover brutality,
That domesticity suffers in slavery.
Girls chosen young to be trained,
Generosity in gestures then feigned.

Beaten badly for petty mistakes,
Minor injuries infected by dictates,
Accidental dexterity can forsake,
Perfection expected for domestic sake.

Hidden dreams sailed at night,
Trapped in dark tunnel groping for light,
A life of slave without any chains,
For hypocrite society's inhuman gains

Roopali Sircar Gaur, Delhi, India

Bittoo: the Boy who lives in the Slum

How to teach that frightened boy with a runny nose
his shorts torn, his belly hungry
Watching his battered mother
inside a dark damp tarpaulin wrapped existence
kicked in her pregnant swell, her hair pulled,
her head crushed
against the brick wall
her screams of anguished pain and at night in the dark
again the violent grunts, and the heavy hurried breathing?
"We mothers must teach our boys to value women. "
The Ladies Club Secretary
declared on Zoom.
growing up in slums and shanty towns
Bholu, Babli, Sonu, Goldy and Bunty

like wriggly worms in cow dung
staring at the carefree neighbourhood college
Pizza, burger eating crowd
The line of cars outside, and the nubile giggling girls
the tight jeans and the T-shirt stretched across
swelling breasts
those unattainable luxuries.

Simmering anger
the brutal existence, the unlettered mind
and the angry voices of men at night
Under the tarpaulin covered brick hutments

Bittoo and his mother sometimes went to the Shiva temple
Where she jostled other women
to lovingly pour milk and flowers
on the dark erect stone phallus.
Her God. His God
Bittoo is learning fast
You see, Bittoo doesn't go to school.
His mother's saree smells of semen
and stale food from Lalaji's kitchen.

Dr Chanchal Sarin, India

STORMS OF LIFE

Sitting in a corner, unheard neglected
Taken for granted
Carrying the weight of her skeleton
Fire coursing through the veins
Heart broken, soul crushed
This is my end, she murmured

Felt dirty, guilty
Tried to pour water on her to clean her body
But the dirt was over her bruised soul
Felt thorns sticking all over piercing her heart
The earth trembling under the feet
Looked for some solace
In the morning crimson rays

I just need to go out of my grid, need a break
Away from all, places, noises, chaos
To find peace, my whole, solace

Let my skin pores be filled with divine calmness
Inhale the air of spring fragrance, she decided
And she left the brick walls

Walking on the hills
In the lush green valleys and the springs
Listening to the echoes of her own voice

A forest, with twists and turns
A pleasant surprise at every turn
The trees smile, and she smiles in return
The flowers greet, become her friends

Swimming like a fish, ever smiling
Reining over the creations
In all layers of ocean
Soothing winds, the abundance around
Nature is my home, she found
The soul awakens, solitude, she felt sound

Storms which disrupted life, also cleared the paths
Moped all sorrows and the guilt in the heart

Sailing through the storms in mind
The negative waves and tides
A new kingdom of thoughts arrives

Life is a mix of joys and sorrows
By thoughts we rise, by thoughts we fall

Rain drops falling from heaven
The blessings of almighty
A cup of tea in her hand, slowly sipping
Sunset has reborn as the next sunrise
And she rises from the ashes

DUST AND HOPE

Sun rises, brings new hope for all
Not for me, my life canvas is dark
Colours are faded, energies drained
No celebrations remain

A bird but wings curtailed
Tongue burnt, eyes blocked, body bruised
Caged in an atmosphere of slavery
I am a wife, must remain in control

My story, rags to riches
Lucky girl, say all dames and bitches
Daughter of poor parents, married to the son of rich
My man suffers from Down's syndrome
The meaning of marriage, not his domain
I have to serve him all my life
An unpaid work, feel is my plight

Silence has descended on me forever
I often smile, a fake one, that must look like real
No escape, my fate, I must bear

I am young, grown like a mushroom
A rose, a radiant beauty
Save the honour of two families, is my duty

My nights are dark, days are grey
Devoid of love, no one to light my way
Dust you are, try not to be a mountain,
was told the other day

The dark clouds enveloping, wish them scatter
Come rain, wash all misty matter
Let the inner glow shine, dark shatter

There was a storm, the other day
Saw the dust rising from the ground
All grains flying free, high towards the sky
Can settle down on oceans, vast expanse, its home
She too felt a storm in her mind, exhales then inhales
Felt she can breathe free, the glow still remains
In the heart, blood still flowing in veins
Finds tranquil solitude in the storm that prevails

Come, like the dust you rise
Fly high, make home wherever you like
On the hills or beyond in the sky
In the rivers, swim or dive
Paint colours on the black canvas bright

Sing the song of freedom, the world is yours,
the words echoed
The self-unfolded its essence
She forgot the past, found self.
Dr. Chanchal Sarin

Pankhuri Sinha, India

The Network of Human Trafficking

Abducted at gun point, drugged and transported
Ever thought of the emotions of the flesh
That runs the brothels? Shines behind the windows
Decorates the neon signs! A shriek can be heard
As rots this flesh, bleeding within the endless trap!
Some were born in it, and were strictly told,
the walls had no doors
From which some actually walked in escaping
the weather n starvation
Rape without compensation! Death n further brutalization!
A stink pervades outside in, and the next time
you casually stop
At the red light signal, and look at the shivering hands
selling the national flag
And the newspapers think of the district called red light,

and what Covid must have done to it!
Did you miss reading about it in your dazed, panicked
corona reports?

Sure! Heartbreaking are the tales of those
tricked by their lovers
Sold in the market, sold like cattle, like slaves!
What never heard of the modern day slavery?
Disguised in form
Masked before the pandemic, keeping the trades
flourishing of prostitution
And its million variants, chat rooms, strip clubs, and even
domestic help
Inside homes with minimal voices! My dears, ever
wondered about the smart
All defying nexus of the human trafficking racket

The Orphan that I am not

No, I am not an orphan
Just the fifth child of that worker
Who works in the brick factory in between the
village and the town?
Stands in the queue before the liquor shop, each evening
I was born perhaps out of one such inebriated rape of my
hungry mother
Who has never known how to protest or resist
Not just his sexual appetite but his beatings
Ever since I was three I have been gathering fire woods
For food to be cooked and never got a full meal!
In the big premises of the buildings
Where I often gather little wooden sticks
The goat herdsman told me, is a school
Its private, but there are schools like that for all
Where with teachings, they give mid-day meal
That night I had a dream! I was a student in uniform
Knowing how to read, write and codify!
Is it true? Can it be?
Can someone rescue? Where is that school?

70

Niharika Chibber Joe, U. S

Breath

"I can't breathe!" wheezed my father
As asthma bowed a broken violin deep within his chest
At 2 a. m. when my mother muttered, "Go!"
I had run in my 14-year-old bare feet to the doctor's home
My bleeding feet were efficient
My father lives.

"I can't breathe!" whined my child
As Delhi's acrid air glazed over his perfectly pink pleura
I raised the car window, and held him close
He fell asleep.

"I can't breathe!" grumbled the defiant 22-year-old
Flinging her cloth mask to the floor
She did not need it to meet friends at the bar
The Virus was not hers to keep

She would hand it off to her friend's father
The beer had been worth it. She was fine!

"I can't breathe!" gasped the friend's father
As the indifferent gurney dumped him onto a bed
Miraculously equipped with a ventilator
That forced air into his labouring lungs
So he could breathe easy.

"I can't breathe!" "Please!"
Wailed a man - a black man
As a cruel white knee pushed into his neck
And held there unflinchingly for eight minutes and forty-
six seconds
Until there was no breath left to breathe.

Mother's Day

Eulogies
So many
Some eloquent, quoting impermanence
Some vacantly verbose
Others mutely peering
From darkened profile photographs
On otherwise vibrant timelines

Eulogies
So many
Even from adult children
Who said they were estranged
From their mother
But, for their mother
They could never
Be strangers

Eulogies
So many
"My mother lost her mind, " they said
"Her mind had gone"
But she had not lost her mind
She had
Lost her children

Sarita Naik, India

Questions

Women, the word resounds on lips
And in many rhymes as flowers
Their eyes as stars and faces as moon
When the body becomes a territory
for man to conquer
Why the battle-line is drawn inwardly?
They are not just purple-blue-birds
For their wings to be broken
But the phoenix to rise from ashes
They grow as sun brightening earth.
As strong currents to cut the stones
And create an ocean, growing strongest ever.
There is hardly any silver-line
for truth to surface

Men and Women an integral part
Of a tree, two boughs
To get sun and water
For fruits and flowers
Still, the matrimonial ads of a girl amuses me
Why?

It is not a Battle

I was told "you are a girl"
And they told my brother, he is a boy
I sit in the veranda and read
"Gender Equality" in a news paper
Preferably a favourite topic for a battle,
The pelting of the summer rain
Circles around me in a sprinkle
I look at my parents, love sits in their nest of heart
Never battling, it lets me free.
There is no one around me for a battle
Nor the world is a battle ground of men and women
But the parallel beams everywhere brightening
In works, in holiday restaurants and in parks
Both are meant to grow and fight
And fight back the storms never retreating
Amidst surging waves as sailors and ships
She wears lipstick not for a girl
But for a boy to burst in praises
For her smile on beautiful lips

Jyoti Sahni, U. S. A

Give me freedom"

Give me the freedom
Freedom to learn
Words and numbers
Attract me more
I am tired of selling
Selling these balloons
O please try to understand
I want to be, who I am
I will work hard
Not here standing on the road

Begging all day long
Words and numbers
Attract me more
I want to learn
Give me freedom
Mother O please do

Wish you a rainbow

We wish for those who cannot see
These beautiful colors of fall we see
Many of us really don't know
The value of existing treasures we have
These two gifts we open in the morning
Wishing the two for everyone we see
We wish them a gift we have
We wish them a beautiful rainbow we see
For what we are thankful
We wish for nothing but others to see.

Padmaja Iyengar-Paddy, India

WOMEN'S DAY

Sister, wife, daughter or mother –
Does she really care or bother,
About what you have
Or what you gave
As brother, husband, son or father?

All she needs is love and peace,
A life of some freedom and ease
Your caring look
From any nook,
Makes her confidence level increase

Do we need a Women's Day?
To say what we have to say?
If you, for her, do care,
Then be willing to share
The joys that came your way

First give women their place.
Respect their eyes and nays.
Understand their needs.
Appreciate their deeds.
Let all days be women's days.

WE BEING WE ...

Are we being rough?
Are we being tough?
Are we being crude?
Are we being rude?

When we say a clear NO
And let the fellow know
That we being WE,
We refuse to be
His Cup of Tea!

Some overtures
By their very nature
Can be repulsive
And be offensive
And cause mental torture

Our smartly built-in antenna
Alerts us to a "certain" agenda
To beware
To be aware
And treat him as anathema

Sriparna Bandyopadhyay, W. B India

Ode to a Bud

That book is not for you,
Do not watch this ad
Alice is waiting there for
You in Wander Land

This soap's for aged folk
Like your granny or so;
Stuart is calling you,
Play with him, just go.

Those dances are not decent,
Will not fit you at all –
Better you play Piano,
Or play with bat and ball.

I preserved your innocence
Building walls of moral;
You want to be an Astronaut;
I know, it's just not verbal.

I make you study hard,
And force you rush to classes
To get you earn reward.
And bathe in pool of success.

On your way back home
In a heat-struck day
Your driver uncle snatched
Your childhood away...

I shielded you, my Tender,
From some Words and Sense
But can't shield, O Dear,
From the very Occurrence

Consistency

It happens every day,
It happens as usual.
Mother earth keeps mum
As if witnessing a ritual

Police has stock pile
Of numerous cases to file,
To finally close as solved –
Resolved or unresolved.

Pen is after the story
Adventure brings some glory
Celebs are on speech.
As long it's in news,
Get focus profuse –
Then just off the switch. . .

'Rape' has many synonyms
All are hackneyed though.
The incidents are so live,
So consistent in flow!

Snigdha Agrawal, India

"TWO FACETS OF HIM"

After a week she returned looking distraught
Eyes missing the shine of a new bride
She slumped on the bed and cried
I asked "what happened to upset you so much?"

Hesitatingly whispered, "He's a monster
Brought up wrong, treats me like Pestle Mortar
Grinding his frustrations to release his anger
And you thought he would be the ideal man for your
daughter"

"The rosy picture you had painted of marriage
Is a far cry from what I've experienced?
Outside facet of the person you were impressed
Inside is filled with rage at his impotence"

"Do you still want me to go back to him?
Continue to be at the receiving end of his ire?
Remain a doormat, subjected to his abusive behaviour
Think over it Ma, and let me know I can remain here"

"I NEVER BELONGED"

Whisked away from the birthing room
Mother informed her child was still born Handed over to
the 'Hijra' group; swaddled in dirty cloth
Just coz my genitals appeared wrong; I never belonged!
In their care I grew up strong, accepting my
fate as they taught
Accepting myself as neither man nor woman;
an in between caught
Swept under the carpet, caste away from mainstream of life
Human privileges denied, left to deal with my fate;
for I never belonged!

My identity lost, half 'nara', half 'nari', of manly physique
Yet in me lived the woman who surfaced on the streets
Dressed as would a lady, flowers in my hair, draped in
saree and blouse
None ever offered employment; begging for alms my only
resort; for I never belonged

They laughed at my demeanor, my quirky looks, my
feminine manners in manly body
Rolled up their car windows to gawk,
at this creature of God

Directed curious looks at me, for in their minds,
I had no gender identity
I am to them, nothing less than a 'monstrosity';
for I never belonged!
©Snigdha Agrawal

Sasha Banhotra, India

Because it was too apt to be a mere act

As performing like every other artist does on stage
Leaping forward sometimes back
Rolling rather gracefully sometimes even hover and
sometimes just lying
On the floor as if making love to it.

I now widen up the spaces
Between them soggy thighs,
so many eyes already analyzing
What must be inside the highs?

As I was playing the victim to my Rapist
My significant other later in the green room
Condemns me for screaming and shouting so good

Claiming it has happened to me before
I beg him to leave and stop as he should
As when asked upon
Why must he think such?
He said, " Because it was too apt to be a mere act, thus. "

And I am left with nothing but shock
As how my love could accuse me of
Something so flawed.
Flawed but aren't the ones lying beneath
It is their body that thumps hers underneath.

I then start thinking of the actual ones
You know the one who received it on a dreary end.
Would my love ever come to know?
The pain I performed is nothing
Compared to them victim's ripping soul
It's gruesome, malice, a rare sin yet so
Not rare in this century whole.

He argued and fought and gave me stares
Those eyes begin to give me less care
He believes it to be true
That I have been raped in truth
The stage was rather crying on my fate
For the message might reach the spectators
But look at the actor's fate!

Easy can never be for women
Her love left her for an act
That she rather performed so marvelous
He still found en error in those
Graceful Shouts and thus
Went off
But doesn't affect her she continues to
Hum the harmony song
Because she is a woman born to perform
She won't stop even if you thump her down, no matter
dusk or Dawn.
© Sasha Banhotra

SOMETIMES I DREAM

Sometimes I dream
And when in the morning
My eyes meet the rays of the darling sun
My psych's already erased the memory
But somehow it still prevails miraculously
In the corners of my brain

I dream, dream and dream
Sometimes about motionless meadows
and sometimes shoutless screams
I dream about being a girl
In strangely quiet afternoons
Leaves rustling echoing through

I see things
Things that are hard to explain
I hear things
Things I wish seemed unheard in a blink

I dream of erasing a few days from the chapters
I do not wish to live any longer
For if I am *"kuch dono ki mehmaan"* under your dome
Let me live before I entirely surrender myself to a Man of
your dreams for me.

Hema Ravi, India

WI (N) DOW UNLATCHES….

Fetters of the turbulent past are broken….
In the silent home, now, his absence haunts!
From deep slumber, she has just awoken
After enduring abuses and taunts

Bird with clipped wings within four walls spent
Sun and Moon rose and set, as did the tides
Never once, against him did she protest
Her creative self - emerged in quick strides

All along, when children studied, she did!
Slowly learnt how to use cutting edge tools
Even though from the public eye, she hid
In time, she gained knowledge of all the rules

Right now, the future stares on vacantly
Fetters of the turbulent past is broken
Unstinting spirit lingers patiently
From deep slumber, she has just awoken!

STIGMATIZED

Many a time during my morning walk,
I encounter them on the roads.
Stopping cars or two wheelers at junctions,
they manage to procure a few notes
Entering shop after other let out a clap,
the cashier from behind his desk
passes on a coin or two.
Sashaying and swaying
I am told the 'taal' is to convey
'I am, who I am!'
Poverty, joblessness, exploitation
has left them in the lurch,
Unable to fulfil stereotypical gender roles
their desire to lead lives of dignity
still unfulfilled......
People are yet to embrace them as they are!

Meher Pestonji, India

Street Girl Among Migrants

She stood apart
Protecting her heart
from the multitude
Thronging free food

Alone she was

Free from the pain
of mothers suckling hungry babies
to dry nipples

Free from the grief
of fathers carrying dying children
on blistered, cracked soles

Free of the confusion
in armies of frightened eyes
fleeing starvation, this side and that

Erect shoulders
breasts covered by tattered dress
legs defiantly astride
saucer eyes staring haughtily
at the unending line

Hungry she was too
but she was used to it
unlike those whose work
was snatched away
at the midnight hour

Her hunger coalesced into anger

Anger had kept her afloat
Against 'goondas', rapists, corrupt cops
Scared off with her acid tongue
Spouting bone-rattling curses
From terrifying gods

Her mission -
to inject her voice
Into kids with sun bleached hair
Matching her own

fill them with the anger
she has known which alone
can be their weapon
to survive.

Venerating Woman

Man's ingenious weapon
– that con-game respect –
chains woman to a pedestal
of 'ma-ji', 'behen-ji', 'devi'
Castrating her right
to anger, rebellion
Sensuality

We fools pluck chains
from Adam's apple tree
to sentence our smiles
for slavery
Ex-pyred

Man
I am
Mother to fire
Sister to water
Goddess with earth and air

A Woman
Standing tall
Questioning all
Conquering all

Renette Peterson D'Souza, Mumbai, India

(Historically, rape or sexual abuse was thought to be, and defined as, a crime committed solely against girls and women, however a large number of cases of raped, sexually abused and assaulted young boys and men still go unreported and victims very often grow up blaming themselves)
Scarred for life

I get chocolate ice cream and all the candy I can eat
He makes me feel most special; being with him
is always a treat
He treats me like his buddy; I am his own little star
We even have our little secrets and bonding
during play hour.
Boys don't cry, Boys don't tell
For what I've done I'm going to hell

How do I say I don't like it, he says I'm his favourite boy
And if I play his game, he'll buy me my favourite toy.

Who am I gonna tell? Will anyone ever believe me?
Alone I carry the shame, ashamed of myself and guilty.
No cuts or bruises to show and tell
Yet Scarred for life, I'm going to hell.

Finding Her Voice

My Voice that lay muffled thru the years
Found its way thru silently wept tears
Where did I come from? Where did I belong?
Was tender and gentle but physically strong
Stuck in the trappings of a male body, that's me
Confused but comfortable in my own femininity
Yet sidelined by society, family and peers
Got marooned in all of its doubts and fears
Robbed of a childhood, given up for good
Never loved by my family, never understood

Uneducated, poor and ostracized
Discriminated against and marginalized
Sold myself to survive night and day
A frustration I fought every step of the way
Struggling to create an identity of my own
To silently fight them demons, I had grown
But not until was I pushed to the ground.
Not until I screamed, that I found
I could fight for my rights, I had a choice
This transgender has finally found her voice.

Sutanuka Mondal, India

The Untouchables

There at the boulevard's end
For the sake of mankind's existence
In shaggy hairs, icky clothes, boots mucky
He keeps your surroundings neat and tidy
His dreams recast to scrubbing soots
Grime, smut, muck, disinfect and floss
Wiping, swabbing from dawn to dusk
Tired yet not, he himself stinks
Soused, blitzed, loud and batty
He stays away from you. . .

You hate his shadow
He makes you puke
Shrouded in poverty
He has nothing to do
The society's Untouchables
He remains aloof
Aloof from you. . .

An Other Sex

When the night falls down and darkness resides
And the streetlights tired of it monotonous job bids bye
His heart murmurs, making him restive
Plethora of memories He or She? Come into his mind.
Crushed by the pressure of his identity
Accompanied by a plaintive cry
Blue or Pink? In a dilemma he sways
Remains always in an unfixable mess
The taunts, debates of 'Thems' and 'Theys'
Question of Third gender, staring eyes on his ways
Society's segregation and injurious notions Shielding up
his gender from all fear and ignorance
Teardrop rolls down from his dejected eyes
While the Hope and Sun shine bright
Starting a day with a fresh mind
With a new spirit he again steps outside.
Singing to be courageous and fine
Propelling the inner strengths to start a day afresh.

Namita Rani Panda, Odisha India

Womb without Womb

Immensely delighted I was feeling my swelling womb
For sprouting a new life within
With the hope of creating a more creative womb
To nurture life beyond!

But alas! My joy shattered!
My womb was ravished by my kith and kin,
My lovable worthy womb was dissected
On the operation table and to garbage was it thrown?

Strangulated was my womb's desire
To see the light and breathe fresh air,
With that ended an era of creation:

End of the womb of womb of womb and so on!
And the result
Imbalance in nature
Now I'm a womb without womb,
A body without soul, a life without life,
A hope without hope,
Impotent! Cursed!

Night after night I listen to her screams of fright,
"Save me! Save me! Save my worthy womb!
Save the womb of my womb!
Save the womb of the universe!"
Can't you hear?

An Unheard Voice

Sitting under the branchless bare tree
Polishing the shoes of the civilized men
In the scorching heat, chilling winter and heavy rain
Making them shine like mirrors
Where I look for my bright future;
But they reflect my dreams stained with
brown and black only
And like my stained hands my future is painted with black
shoe polish.
My hopes mutilated like the branches of the bare tree,
My eyes like the lenses of a binocular
Long to embrace the grand life beyond my reach.
The men in cars with gaudy dresses,
The children in shoes, uniforms and schoolbags
Ignite me to dream unreachable dreams.
Don't have I the right to dream?
Why do you call my dream a mirage?
Why is my voice unheard?
My foggy future is moving confidently towards dark night,
Please do something to stop him!
Please respond to my unheard voice!
I' m waiting anxiously.... !

Satabdi Saha, India

WOMAN

Your fiery whiplash of stringed words,
aimed at demeaning me,
Can't scald the firmly stemmed will,
nor ash that rose, blooming each day,
Fed inside, with light and rains, thorn-shielded
My raging flame dissolves your iced rock
daring to force deeply dark,
To shred petals, reducing it to shivers,
like cold waters in winter nights.
Ego- tyrannies fail to press on wishes,
steeled by oppression,
Even though my mud house collapses and I'm up,
to necking high waters.
My hollow nourishes flesh, to be breasted; even patriarchy,
At its crudest. . . . abandoned, you could've died hungry

Puny, vulnerable baby! Even if I know what you'd be,
Tender mask hides an innate sadist.
Yet love, my strongest weakness, still flunks me.
Tricks don't play always. Genuine feelings burgeon, both
sides.
Or children. So I sweet- shackle myself,
Enslaved
Happy slavery! Often forever enslaved even if yours ebb.
Yet, torture, suppression, denials, oppression race
And has been for centuries, Fear Factor
You know, I was and am more than even with you.

I, the Archetypal Woman!
Race me, but you cannot attain - a mother's joy in a
birthing pain.

GODDESSES

Inside a brick construct darkness
Mothers' dark
A scented paddy field of unripe years,
Overwhelmed by stench of putrid game
Stories of redness on green – unfolds.
The hot virgin sky flushes out shades of crimson
Sunny malignant on burial grounds
Of screams—throttled by lust of centuries
Torn legs, slit throats – run through the centre
Of the city. Beastly propriety Demands
Do not unclothe before devouring.
A car moves, cigarette smoke, heads jostled—
The crying earth receives – a kick-out,
Lacerated, worm eaten- a no- body-a lady said,
'No character'—nothing to think about.
The mad woman in the tower roars—
No, no, contrived – The mad woman with a whip
Chides, go, Sen. , go- where truths are told—
Then no screens—that face--many faces
Mingled thousands, — 'No, no, not anymore—'
Why do we worship clay goddesses! The cycle begins again.

Misna Chanu, India

WHEN YOU DID THAT TO HER

When you twisted her wrist
Or hit on her face, dear men!
Did you ever notice -?
How her self-respect was twisted,
And her dignity was broken into pieces!

Did it ever cross your mind? -
Yes! The thought of what you did to her!
Yes! To her, the one; who had left everyone?
And almost everything she used to call her own,
Since she arrived on this land, we call Earth,
To be with you, to live with you
And to make a world of you two!

She might not able to make your world
As heaven as you dreamt,
She might not be perfect in many fields of life
As you expected her to be,
Because she's a human just like you,
Not a goddess or angels from heaven,
Neither a property nor artifacts you own!

But ask yourself! Oh! dear men!
Did you ever care to make her feel?
That she was loved, wanted and valued in your world?

Namramita Banerjee, India

FIFTEEN OR CLOSE

In the long dark silent street
She tripped and fell as she tried to run,
Got up again without a thought
She stepped blindly on dry leaves.

Someone chased her throughout
From one street to other,
She tried seeking help from all
But they all were muted stones.

Stop! Stop! I can't run more
Her body kept trying to give up,
But her heart and mind knew very well
That her way had no exit

It was all grey and black
Her eyes ached to see some light,
But she knew she had no option
Run! Run for life and don't turn around.
But her fate seemed to be hard
The man who followed got hold of her,
Pinned onto the ground she yelled for help
Her voice echoed in every corner but no one turned.

Her heart bled that night
With her body and dignity
Laid on the road like a crushed bud of rose
She was just fifteen or closed!

Let Her Be

Oh, she is too skinny!
Oh, she is too fat!
Look she is pretty
But she is a prat!

She has got the perfect curves
But she is a hooker;
Oh, she is too manly
With a skin so darker!

You shame her for her shape
And for her skin,
You shame her for her ways
As if she a sin.

Whether it's her arms or calves
Or her thighs with marks,
She is constantly criticized
Which takes away her sparks?

The freckle on her face
Is not her fault?
She is a human like you
She cannot be perfect in all.

She can be fat or skinny
Doesn't need to fit in,
Also, pretty and funny
Let her shine from within.

Let her just be a harsh stain
Of vibrant colours on a canvas,
She just wants to live
A life with purpose

Srutakirti Tripathy, India

Death of a transgender

The entire neighbourhood was buzzing!
A transgender has lost its life
Not without food
Rather lack of respect
Taken aback, its tender life

In anxiety of listening the word 'Mother'
One midnight,
She brought an unwanted child home
Nurtured him with great affection
Building a nest of divine love

Can ever a transgender be mom?
Such rough words of hatred
Everyday shattered her endurance

Still she bears all agony
Always being remained silent

This gentle society one day
Taken away,
The last hope of his survival
Next day, the news prevailed
A transgender died out of hunger.

My dream

I have a dream
To watch a changed India
Where women remain safe
Instead of mercy and sympathy
With respect they would grace.

Will the candle march?
Return their precious life?
If ever people have the sensitivity
Would women lose their pride?

After few days 'hollow discussion
Peoples' sympathy fade
Life become normal and as usual
But the issue is still the same.

Dignity of women would untouched
Let her bloom and flourish
No beast could spoil her life
Treating poor, weak and helpless

Sonia Ghosh, India

Unstoppable

Morning or evening he is there
Student, aged, employee all are hailed
Bombastic words, political colloquy
Make his brows up and down
He carries papers with unknown letters

On one murky morrow
His immature fingers handling tray
A college-goer late riser, nudged.
Then a beer belly came with a wooden cane
To give him lessons and intolerable pain
A dodderer told "now we're same ",
Seeing him limping with the kettle and blame

Moon gathered all, flamed firecrackers of words,
Again a running bicycle met.
He jumped, was saved but not safe.
The last straphanger came for a sip
he again hobbled for service

Not he alone, there are many, uncountable,
We know only one vicinal limping tale.

Room-key

She was filling the glasses,
Suddenly rushed to the mirror,
Brushed some rouge more.
Welcoming him with filled one
He sipped a little while unhooking
loosened her dress...
She grasped the bed sheets with her fists.
He went on till he zipped,
Had some chips and tightened the shoes.
Threw some coloured papers on the bed

Another one entered,
She tightened her dress.
The weary eyes whispering 'no'
But the crumpled prescriptions made her go
He locked the door with a smile
She went to the mirror again
She grasped the bed sheets once more

Dr. Megha Bharati 'Meghall' India

"Men are from Mars
Women are from Venus"

That's what I've always heard
While growing up

But. . . while growing up -
On this Earth,
I also have realized. . .
This Earth is where I belong to
and no place else...

I was born free here, crying loud,
Making unobstructed sounds

so why now! Would I live in chains?
Why should I design cocoons to survive?
and give up to restraints ?

I want to live here free. . .
free like a human should be.
free from the bars of colours,
free from this criterion
of pink and blue.

free from this viciousness of the world
that derides and says-
oh! he's feminine
oh! she's masculine

I want to love,
want to say
want to live. . .

I want to live free
and make this earth a place -
where. . .
there are no boundaries to a woman's loving heart
there are no restrictions to a man's loving mind
there are no limitations to the loving human kind

'cause this earth is where I belong to
and no place else.
So let them now say-

Men are from Mars
Women are from Venus
But with identities tightened
with strong girth,
Here rises the selfless genus,
Providing plenitude of space,
Plenitude of power for all
No dearth!
'cause
"Humans are from Earth".

"More than ever. . . "

Let there be happiness in the air,
and feel it more than ever,
let there be equality all around,
and adhere to it more than ever.

let there be love,
selfless, empowering,
and share it more than ever.

let there be sturdy bodies,
not feminine, not masculine,
let there be attraction more than ever.

let there be attire's & adornments for all,
not only pink, not only blue,
let there be colours more than ever.

let there be freedom to express hearts, freedom
to express mind's,
and let them express more than ever.

let there be children, men, women, transgender,
homosexuals, bisexuals and pansexuals,
let there be humans,
let there be humanity,
and weave it more than ever.

Boby Bora, Assam India

Zest for Newness

While moving ahead,
amidst the cacophony,
leaving the woods behind.
My feet
was entrapped by a root.
Gradually, as it was about to grab my chest;
I gained consciousness.
Tried to disentangle the roots
and break free.
In the course of the undying attempt,
to free myself,
from the clutches of the roots;
have lost some valuable moments

in new indulgence.
Warm tears
rolled down.
Those silent moments
while in search for fragrance,
have meandered
in an uneven speed,
towards the stark darkness.
While on the verge of being lost,
you clasped my hands.
I took two steps forward ----
with profound confidence ;
with the warmth of the new sun----
towards the valley of spring,
towards the path of light,
with the new gained consciousness.
©® Boby Bora

Does the River Speak?

The continuous flowing river,
cautiously carries in its heart;
murmurings of some dreams.
The turtle lying still on the sand;
quivers, as the rays of the early sun,
fall on its back.
The silver fishes peeps.
The pale leaf of the green tree,
falls silently,
Surreptitiously...
The stone gathers marks of ageing.
The silver ripples
of the golden mermaid's giggles,
brings back life
to the heart of the lifeless river.
Again, the torrential surge;
shatters the shimmering dreams
of mother's eyes.
Some cheerful youth
loses his tune,
while being in tune
with the song of his life.
The cartilaginous fish
writes vehemently,
in the heart of the stone,
that lies in the river bed,

about the trials and tribulations,
of the shattered dreams,
of the green pathways.
How will the river express?
that if not clutched within its core;
the greens will remain untouched,
by the silt;
and will fail to spread
the golden smile.

The Elixir Of Life

What does life grant?
What death takes away?
The one who snugs on a warm cozy bed;
embraces the cold crude stretcher for eternal rest.
Thousand dreams of those alive,
becomes the cobwebs of death.
Life's exacting whirlpools,
its stone heavy burden.
Those numerous poisonous arrows
that pierces through the heart.
The red pigment of the blood
turns colourless
An empire transforms into its catastrophic remains.
The pinnacle of youth,
its endless glories
seeks its last refuge
unto something divine.
The truth of life:
Life is beautiful,
Life is 'Shiva'
Death is just
an ice-cold sensation,
of the ultimate journey;
The ultimate refuge,
for the eternity

Kanta Roy, India

Impotence Of Nation

Who cries in the bush (!)
Who is the girl dead (!)----
A different heart beat heedeth much in
Roadside vehicles dousing petrol engines flirt;
hunting diary of an innocent flowers
night›s muscle fearful about witty
postures sendeth mercy on a innocent
breath's soaker
o, yes, girls are dearly birds and how
Sweetened made womanly error more
Easily woman breathing mothership
wombs
are they birds(?)
Can they wing chose freedom (?)
Or bread of lustre and

helpless heart to be in slayed for
amazement underworld !
how youths can have dark sex evening
how many holy field loosen globe's names
how they drinketh lustre and tasteth
blood
how doth feel food field forestry shalt be era steals
they art blind by narcotic addiction
some art mental patients
some for social injustices
some knowest as addiction
to porn bites ;
swalloweth female, mouth open door,
run by loosen bones lay down
a disease carries out society,
where shrinking all morality, and weeping
humanity in blind errors rudiments :
so much we need angelic
a proper sex - education and
needeth morality to simplify
the secrets of Anatomy and
Wellness of proper adulation.

Sujata Paul, Tripura India

Ugly

She was in pain at her abdomen
Trying to stand up but unfortunately fell down...
Trying to remember something what actually happened
But!
burst into tears then!
That day on the way back from her college
She had gone somewhere with one of her
friends to have a job
To assist her widow mom financially
That guy by the name of giving job
Taken her by a car
Where some other teenagers looking
panicked had been there
Then after forcing them to get down from the car

They had been to a single room under the star...
Only to be gang raped in the darkness of that night.
Suddenly in front of her eyes appeared the ugliest civilized
society's sight

Would Like To Suggest

They say that I am the transgender…
No idea why have I been created such by the sender?

Neither there is any fixed family or address of mine
Nor I can spend any quality time anywhere
in the social line

Whenever I get in any car or train…
People avoid me and sometimes try to tease me in vain.

Even the dear and near ones behave the same
Hence seeking the assistance of Government even without
any shame

To have handful of food I rush to the people's houses
Whenever any celebration take place

If they don't help spontaneously I have to insist them
Is it my destiny or born to be ashamed

Hence would like to suggest my next generation's third
gender to stand against this evil system,
And tide over all these issues being learned
with righteous frame

Deepti Mohapatra, Odisa, India

EVERYDAY STRUGGLE TO EXIST

Because he is a man…
Every day he fights for his existence. . .

Lending a helping hand every time questions his character
Because he is a man…
Every day he fights for his existence. . .

For some shameless beings his masculinity became fierce
Because he is a man
Every day he fights for his existence. . .

His hard work for family always count the sweat he burn
each day but every time the stereotype speaks and he falls
Because he is a man
Every day he fights for his existence. . .
Whenever he opts to his choice, he was laughed and criti-
cized for his sensitivity
Because he is a man
Every day he fights for his existence. . .

Every time he had to hide his emotions, his cries, his heart
aches
Because he is a man
Every day he fights for his existence. . .

A thought of expressing his feelings towards someone,
doubts for lust above love
Because he is a man
Every day he fights for his existence. . .

Sometimes he is also tired and broken, what if, he shout,
get angry still he is a human to speak his heart out, is it not
you to understand him, then who else shall he show his
rights but all it states aggression and a reason to complain
Because he is a man
Every day he fights for his existence. . .

If someone expects him to bring a diamond ring, the one should also know the everyday exhaustion he bear but that someone will never know

Because he is a man

Every day he fights for his existence. . .

NO. . .

I said No
I was pulled off. . .
I said No
I was slapped. . .
I said No
My mouth closed tight. . .
I said No
My dress got torn. . .
I said No
My body got bruises. . .
I said No
I got choked. . .
I said No
I am strangulated. . .
I said No
I got burned. . .
I said No
I was buried. . .
I said No
I am gone. . .
I said No
My soul is insistence. . .

Baishakhi Chakraborty, India

Tale of a Girl Child

A girl child born in a traditional middle class joint family
None welcomed her with the sound of
conch or oil-lamp gaily
All expected a boy who will look after parents at old age
So treated her like an ignored bird in a forlorn rust-cage.

The biggest piece of fish or mutton given to her brother
She hides her sigh from childhood knowing her gender
Her brother gets all opportunity to play and study joyfully
She helps her mother in household jobs at free time daily

All expensive dresses, all costly toys given to her brother
She gets all used things of her siblings to fulfill her desire

On birthday brother gets lucrative
gifts luminous celebration
No one gives a single toffee or a doll on
her special occasion.

She works very hard in daytime after
household work complete
At night studied in light of lantern
when whole house asleep
With a focus of furious fume she wants to be a doctor
Her frustration become her weapon
to reach goal of nectar

At last she passed out successfully, a gold medal won
Now for the first time her parents gave her recognition
She's a doctor who treat her old
parents as brother abscond
Her education, her honour, her performance give
full recollection. . .

Hussein Habasch, Kurdistan /Germany

Weeping

She wept in the morning
She wept at noon
She wept in the evening
At morning she lost a son
At noon she lost another
At evening she lost the last of family
In the next morning they cried for her
At noon they cried for who were crying for her
At evening there were no remaining cries
The whole town was swamped with blood.
Translated by MunaZinati

A flying angel

The child whom they tied her broken hands
In white gauze
She urged her mother to know
Why her hands are tied like that?
When the mother became confused and
couldn't find an answer
She whispered to her: my little one, you became an angel.
Is it not true the angels have white wings?
The little one believed her mother
Slowly, she is recovering
Moving her hands like wings
And trying to fly
Translated by MunaZinati

Mircea Dan Duta, Romania

Victoria 1 Sum

I am the one that is only equal to itself,
but different from its own identity,
I am the one breaking the balance of the landscape
seen with both eyes
I am the one adding an a before the word symmetrical,
I am the one because of which one can't say one's prayer
until the end,
for I am neither the Father, nor the Son and I'm not al-
lowed to pretend
I'd represent something holy; let it be a spirit or a ghost.
I am the one nobody wants to have children with,
even if I were able to give birth to children.
I am fat when anyone else is white,
I am black when anyone else is clever,

I am stupid when anyone else is brutal,
I am oversensitive when anyone else is slim,
or by reverse,
I was not born a woman, even if everyone else is able to
become one,
or by reverse,
I am the Different one, different from you, different from
her, different from him,
I am the Unlikely one,
I am the Third one,
so don't tell me I'm beautiful, for you know I'm not
and I know I am
Original language: Czech

Translation into English:
Judit Antal & Corina Oproae

Silent Night II (There, at the Final Station)

I'm not going to be your Christmas Tree
I won't allow you to cut me off my roots with
your human axe,
to steal my dead body from the forest,
to bring it to your warm & cosy human home,
to fasten it next to your warm & friendly human oven,
to put on it some immaculately white human dress,
to make me your beloved human bride
and to replace my mortal wild existence
in the pagan forest
with a human life that may become immortal
after my next human death
if I manage to avoid temptation to sin.
I am not going to be your Christmas Tree.
It's about time for you to learn
Christmas Tree is a Gender Neutral,
not a Feminine, and for sure not a Common Noun.
A Christmas Tree just doesn't feel like being decorated
according to your taste.
A Christmas Tree just doesn't feel like being decorated.
A Christmas Tree just doesn't feel like
being someone's Christmas Tree,
A Christmas Tree just doesn´t feel like
being a Christmas Tree at all.
For you, a Christmas Tree is just a pretext for keeping
alive the illusion

of being able to make something more beautiful than it is.
But how could you embellish something you killed in order to embellish?
How could dead beauty add beauty to a beauty that is already dead?
I am not going to be your Christmas Tree.
I won't become the topic of some stupid human stories of yours.
And if on Christmas Day you find me lying down on the sidewalk,
buried under the snow that has fallen the whole night
on the little square at the final stop of the city train,
remember I have never been your Christmas Tree,
for I choose to be someone else's.
Nevertheless,
if you really care so much about Christmas Trees,
you can always buy yourself an artificial one
and order a personalised Christmas during the first week of January,
before the death of the Three Wise Men.

Original language: Czech
Translation into English: Judit Antal &
Corina Oproae

Maid Corbic, Bosnia and Herzegovina

WOMEN DESERVE FREEDOM

They were born queens, not workers
Give them freedom to the world, you men are
pathological liars
Which you can't wait to see the benefit of them
So you sell them as slaves usually to someone else
Let it be an honor and a shame, heroes!

Women deserve freedom and the right to move
That no one restricts them because of their position
Equality should be in every possible field
One should give them freedom and
believe in sincere words

This is directed by that very person, 'the WOMAN'

Women deserve freedom because it really matters
Imagine constantly monitoring them like a guard dog
So when he rejects you, don't get mad at the world
Because she turned to herself now, not to you!

Women deserve freedom, not trade over them
Because they still have the right to vote for the rebellion
All the power you have in you is useless, if you are not
human
Let the woman live her life, you deserve
confession with God
You will pay dearly for every mistake!

DOMESTIC VIOLENCE

We suffer that violence that happens to us in the family
We hide the beatings so that other people can't see us
What a life we actually live, because we have an abundance
of everything
But in vain when the soul is not full
And when you spend every night around the
corner of the room !?

Like a dog literally hanging on a chain imaginary
You suffer everything that the other side
does to you violently
You shed tears, but it doesn't help you much
When you feel pain in the area of your spine
Buried with a sharp knife
Domestic violence must not be silenced
Because eventually everything is actually revealed
It is better to prevent than to cure
When it becomes too late to correct mistakes
Because then everything becomes just ashes and dust!

Isaac Cohen, Israel

The Scars

The child screamed…
"All the scars you made me
with belt buckle far away
from your light years
Go to hell. "
©All rights Reverved

Stop the Murder

Loran Haton be an old bachelorette
Her neighbored asked her:
When did you get married?"»
Loran lowered her eyes and whispered:
"What God will decided be happen. "

One day.
The voices of joy come to the neighborhood.
Loran got married with a divorced man.
He had a kid, ten years old.
All the people happy

One year later.
The hushed sound appeared:
He hit her. "»
A naive women that
Whispered to the dragonflies was
beaten and injured
My body felt battered
Oh God, »
Please
stop the murder!"

Fareed Agyakwah, Africa

Diminutive Dandelions

Diminutive dandelions-
They grow regardless
Of the soil
They rise in spite
Of crudest conditions
Meted out to them
Life bares its teeth as rabid dogs
At their little lives
Who else is responsible?
In the face of neglect's stalk,
Abuse's charge, poverty's pounce,
Diminutive dandelions-
They bounce as football
Back from hardest pitches.
Because diminutive dandelions

Are the eye-egg of God:
So tell those who beat, bat, bang
The hell out of them that they are in for wrath
Children aren't punching bags
But our little selves

Child Abuse

From where we woke, my brother
Child abuse's like potable water
On the back of a duck

When the beast in men go wild,
On the squashy cheeks of a child
Elderly hands weirdly lands.

In their bid to love as asses love to bray
And care for puny souls that knows not their way
Our elders refuse to disabuse.

They ride on the back of The Word
With flabby flesh feeding rod
Inflicting pain for senseless gain

Developmental delay's all you see;
Suicidal thoughts source the sea
In feeble little children

The sea overflows its shores;
The child becomes timid, of course.
Only the insane will count it gain.

Monsif Beroual, Morocco

Between the lines

Between the lines, the rhythm of love reborn
When their smile tells everything
When their wonderful heart explain anything,
I hear the rhythm of innocent love
That wants to set free one day without chains.
Paint the world, color it with a love song;
A symphony of this colorful song reaches my soul,
Where I've been lost between the mysterious lines,
Between the happiness sort his sinful ink.
I hear the rhythm of love, like a symphony plays a
sinful tune,
When the words become alive
And the feelings reach our heart
Do we need to surround for this love?
That burns our heart for the world it's wrong
But for the soul and heart, nothing is wrong.

Love is love, has no color or skin,
Only pure feelings that reach our heart;
It's the symphony of love
When you see the world through your heart,
not your eye,
The rhythm of love reborn within the lines of
poetry heart
© MONSIF BEROUAL

BUTTERFLY SOUL

Shall I fall like a leaf broken to pieces for long nights?
Or to ignore this colorful song
That made my life meaningful with your existence,
That illuminates my dawn.
I wrote a wish while the leaves fall
Made of eternal magical letters
To spell it for a lifetime
Asking for eternity place into your heart
Wished if I can hold it for a while
But with the distance it was a hard to reach,
It might be our souls are stronger enough to sneaks
Trying to reach that a noble desire as a butterfly soul,
Because within every breathe
I miss you before we've meet
And I feel you without watching your tears fall.
I built this new world to keep you inside
As the valve holds the balance of my heart
To not fall for suicide end
But In both ends I'll be alive within your heart
For eternity sake

K. V. Dominic, India

Anand's Lot

Anand's eyes were immersed
on pupils in tempting uniforms;
Longed to be one of them again
How happy were those days!
Mummy gave me kiss and ta-ta
and like butterflies flew to school
with Rajesh, Praveen and Smitha
chattering, singing, dancing, running.
Alas! Like a vulture came the car then;
picked me in and dashed away.
A bearded-man with a black towel
hushed my helpless wail for help;
brought into a house and shut in a room.
I was fed with cold dry bread and slept on floor dead tired.
Car picked me in morning and brought to this strange city.

They removed my dress and dressed me in rags.
They threatened to kill me if I disobeyed their orders.
I have to sleep in their hut, eat dry bread which I hate;
always wear this stinky rags. They scold me and beat me
for not earning much through begging as they dreamed.

International Women's Day

International Women's Day;
Celebrations all over the world;
Meetings held; programs chalked out;
Promises showered; fund allotted;
Celebrities honoured; her praises sung hoarse
Coarse in her life's course
Mockery's rhetoric in these celebrations!
All echoes of years of yore.
Problems remain the same!
Birth to death, an instrument of lust
and hot-selling sex.
Her very birth ill omen: an unwelcome event.
No guilt in foeticide; foeticide is matricide;
No life without mother. Sexism in childhood;
Priority to her brother; her food, his leftover
Chained in kitchen, she rarely goes out.
No toys, no plays; always envies him.
Mum and dad love him; she gets only reproaches;
beat her very often. Seldom educated;
hence no employment, and always dependant.

Alan Cherian Puthenpurayil, India

Freedom of Speech

My pen has the right to speak,
To raise voice against all the atrocities,
To revolt against all the inequalities
And to give hope for the larger human needs

It tells the story of the leveraged lives
Wherein hunger has to play a role
Oppressed beings are my characters
Who wish to remain as shadows?

Shadows too speak
But it hardly reaches the ears of authority.
The blind eyes of power neglects them
In a rush for name and fame

To instill a hope in them,
To wake and to dream
Fighting for our own rights
Is the base of any revolution?

Boundaries and binaries are never bliss
Yet bestowed forcefully,
They can either be a shadow
Or else a mirror to reflect

Cradle in Borders

The sound of battleships,
Rifles and explosions
Are lullabies and appeasement
For her ears

The smoke, fume
And the dust
Are worldly fragrances
For her

The thunder, lightning
And the cyclones
Are now
A daily routine

Her eyes are shuttered
And her ears are sealed
Death and chaos
Wriggles before her
Missions and machines
Dance before her.

Calamities and disasters
Run after her
Nothing is unusual
Before her eyes

Khesise Lungma, Bhutan

Children and women Abuse

Why abuse children and women with black attire
When everyone sons and daughters always fear.
Hiding them under shade of harassment and tear
Families and friends feel heavy at heart to bear.

Please understand they are made of flesh and bones
No men or women of brutal heart must kidnap thee
They are our citizens of country, who works like bees,
They are our young flowers that makes society clean.

Implementing integrating efforts to subdue violence
Are best protections for children and women in silence?
Eliminating the silos of habitual realms of maltreatment
Let us protect physical torture, the mental harassment.

Why abuse children and women with yearning desires
To make them play under your

darkened mind to perspire,
Yours punishment and hard labour will crack their bones
threatening under fear shelter with pain not able to moan.

Why sporadic or harassment on children and women?
That results severe depression or anxiety for human.
Both faces double jeopardy in terms of behaviors mind
Physically and mentally they get disorganized at sights.

MD Ahtesham Ahmad, India

I'm a gender too!

First gender, second gender
Like them I'm a third gender.

Nature has made me what I am
Doesn't it mean a human I too am?

Deprived I remain in every aspect
Society robs me of worthy respect

Denied right to work in an institution
I am forced to enter into prostitution

I go begging in every bus and train
Folks look upon me with utter disdain

I throughout my life stay uneducated
As my life everywhere is unprotected

You genders! Give me my human right
I much like you can fight with all might

Tale of an Eve

I am a baby- a baby in my babyhood.
Why in me do you see womanhood?
Let me grow up and identify myself.
Let the woman in me meet herself.

A daughter, a sister, a wife, a mother,
Sometimes I take the role of a father.
Preying on me you abuse all kinship
And make me go through all hardship.

When the life for Adam was solitary,
God created Eve as Adam's only fairy.
The two words 'wife' and 'man' joined.
That's how the word 'woman' is coined.

An Eve does make your life worth living.
Like you Adams, Eves are human being.

To all Eves here, respect must be given.
For Eves are wonderful gifts of heaven.

Tapankanti Mukherjee

Blackhole

Krishna is supposed to board the bus from
This stop…
Every day she waits here after the office
And picks up dreams while waiting…
When the bus comes,
Krishna shoves herself into it.
Standing or sitting, she burns with the
Desire of male touch
Now she is haunted by fears instead of dreams
When she gets into the bus, she feels creeping
Into a cave
The body burns, the mind vibrates in fear.
The royal road witnesses constant candle procession.

But the mystical feeling, the fresh rhythms
Of life stifle
Apart from the smoky smell,
The Krishnas breathe in nothing in these days

Cloud - colour

Water bubbles in the tea - kettle
Sushama stares at it.
The still illusory of gas, the collage of cloud
And sunshine, the unsteady north wind,
Cyclone storms in the mind of Sushama.
Why only the women are to suffer always?
Time teaches a lot.
Does then time mean experience?
Sushama starts licking the past.
One river encroaches upon her eyes
Full to the brim
The kettle overhears and survives
While being in space.
Sushama extinguishes the stove
And pours a lump of void in the cup
While muttering

Bagawath Bhandari, Bhutan

Thy Daughter...

I am an art,
Of thou heart,
Born on the earth,
To bask the warmth of thy hearth

I am a daughter,
Wanting to get filled with laughter,
But I am scared of monsters,
Roaring behind me akin to the thunder

I am afraid to walk at night,
For those monsters waiting for fleshy fight,
And I keep locking myself in the room,
Desolated, haunted and doomed.

I am a prey of those ill humans,
But they are filled with the highest acumen,
And I keep worrying about my life,
Strolling on the path of sadness and grief

I am a daughter of mother earth,
And I want to feel her beating heart,
Protect me and my generation of girls,
Attending their humanly calls.

I am Black...

I am torn apart,
And I walk solo with broken heart,
As I am outcaste by the color I wear,
Getting sodden in the pool of my tears

I am black, Yes, I am,
But I am fine,
With the color that I wear on my skin,
Amid darkness I design my own scene.

I wear the color of earth,
And I possess the heart,
That beats for humanity,
Peace and Tranquility.

I am black in color,
But I bloom akin to flower,
Radiating every corner of world,
In the warmth of my huggable folds

Give me a little space to live,
Devoid of any sorrow and grief,
And respect the color that I wear,
And I want to endure with no tear and fear.

Shubhashish Banerjee

Beyond the bias

In a nation where the girl child is deified
As the revered 'Devi', Goddess Supreme
And worshipped by devotees with relentless esteem
Why is she denied a place in Mother's holy abode,
Deprived of Her benison, benediction and gleam ?
Just because she was born the subtle girl on earth
Religious doctrines formulated at her birth
By incestuous guardians of society corrupt
Confining her, tormenting her, depriving her of her rights
deserved
With masculine ruthlessness in the mind reserved
Why not shed the prejudices of a lifetime ?

Why not let her retain the quintessential luster and shine ?
Women weave the civilization we reap
So why make our righteous women weep ?
Mothers, daughters, sisters and the wife
We look to them for solace during strife
Those committing atrocities on their women folk
Talk of stagnant tradition old
Aren't you a disgraceful lot claiming to be bold?
Venerate the divine feminine, treat her alike without preju-
dices cold.

Don't abuse her silence

Women are not commodities to be displayed and used
For petty commercial gains portraying gaudy hues
Beauty lies in the soul in furtive grace
All nudity crude is a slap on the face
On assertions of all the decent cognizance we boast of
Women abuse is abuse of the birth of an individual
Tainting one's origin, blemishing the creative quintessential
From holy matrimony to the dens of prostitution
Exploiting women has become an organized institution
Lethal in its endeavor to choke and suppress voices un-
heard
Power is a perpetrator of crime continuous
Heraldry in its boast sounds vociferous
Subduing the voice of women they say
Their mothers and daughters constitute their family
of dreams
While the male ego nefarious tramples upon their instincts
in repugnant memes
Dreams shall be materialized when women come on
their own
Churning and spurning the vituperation of victimization
With a rebellious tone
Don't take her existence for granted undermined
Vengeance is her cry for victims lined.
Â© Shubhashish Banerjee

182

Sankha Ranjan Patra, India

Woman

Woman underestimated
Woman mistaken
Though the leader of a nation
Though the leader of a family.

Woman worshipped
Woman disgraced
The earth becomes Heaven
The earth becomes Hell.

All the sacrifices
Incomparable
All the determinations
Indomitable

All the troubles
In vain
All the struggles
In pain
Her affection without condition
Her dedication an inspiration

Innocence

Robbed before my eyes
Innocence that lies
When I run through the lane
made by ignorant man.

Images of exploitations
captured without intentions
When I have to run
On the way to earn.

If past an instance of gloom
Future then gives in to doom
Secured childhood offers
This lands so many toppers.

A child of to day
A father of tomorrows
A man in small size
Becomes so wise

This stage must be nourished
So that it can be flourished
Maybe many a blank paper
Waiting for a beautiful cover

Orbindu Ganga, India

DOWNTRODDEN

Days are scented with sweating drops
Toiling with the Auburn,
Onlookers gave a sly smile
Seeing the apathy in broad daylight
Being born to the less privileged
The society showed empathy
With a glance of discrimination,
Ages can flow with time
Exploiting the innocence shall remain,
Old wines are refilled
With the venom, evincing disparity,
Each drop becoming volatile
For the others to relish,
Unknown about the harsh realities

Faced by the downtrodden,
Some gazelles with no hearts
Only to realize late, being optimist in life,
Never to realize the mistakes committed
Many still saunter in search of prey
Seeing the desolated destroy their conscience.

BEING A TRANSGENDER

Being discerned in society
For being the self, being the form,
The tears have no value
For the heartless living in the commune,
Being targeted every time for
Being different, being another species,
Born with a smile to love the world
Living with a smile hiding the tears,
Heart crawls to find the space
To be in solitude, away from the crowd,
Animals are adorable humans
Giving us love when given the care,
Humans have left humanity
Trying to cease the tag of a social animal
To become the animal,
Being insensitive to fellow humans
To become the beast,
Humans are becoming a threat
To humanity, creating disharmony
Being the species inviting extinction.

ParashuramRao Gande. India

Stand for the Weak

Let us think of the rag pickers
Waking up early in the morning
Holding baskets in their left hands,
Picking up the left over and used liquor bottles
Empty and consumed water bottles
Empty plastic tins
Searching for cut and left over iron pieces
Of iron rods at construction sites
They continue to roam amidst houses
The rag pickers girls and boys in tottered clothes
Appear in every street and every day
For some means to live at any cost
Let us stand for them

And by them and fight for their rights
Helping them join the main stream
Like the small tributaries entering in to the main rivers
They need education and financial support
The governments and the rich must do
Not with sympathy but with empathy.

Abuse of the Innocent Children

Small children who are in helpless condition
Who have become orphans by cruel fate?
Who are abandoned by hapless poor parents?
Generally lured to work in the rich houses
As domestic servants for meager salaries
For hand to mouth existence
They work endless and without proper rest
Without proper medication when needed
The children who run away from their homes
Unbearable of the miseries caused by drunken parents
Also work as domestic helps
Their lives are like disconnected kites
The poor abandoned girls sometimes forced to
Work in the prostitute houses in the red light areas
Middle men tempt them to join the prostitute houses
Under the pretext of earning money by them
Thus the under aged unfortunate children,
Thus the hapless girls and boys are abused by the
Malicious persons who spoil the children by
their evil designs

Ayodhyanath Choudhary, India

Nipped in the Bud

She is absolutely like a flower
Is there any difference?
Only softness, only tenderness
Simply a body of reverence.

Everyone wants to pluck her
Ignorant of any danger
Is plucking really loving?
What a foolish plunderer!

What a beautiful smile!
Must it not remain?
The foolish do not mind
What vile doing will gain!

Let her offer fragrance
Let the mild wind blow.
Every flower is neutral
Don't mar the glow.

Her redness must attract
Don't let it ever die.
Beauty is only to see
Believe! O foolish guy!!

Don't nip in the bud
Just feel pleasure.
Enjoy life within you
In boundless measure.
(Copyright reserved with the writer)

Abhijit Chakraborty, India

My sad sky

My sad sky covers my face with that gesture of sadness
My gray sky weeps in the desert Sahara
My sky is stuck in a small window
Darkness and sorrow are firmly attached
There is no moon in this sky,. . no sun. . no dream. . no
rhythm. . no color. . no smell !
There are only birds that sing sad songs
My two eyes stay awake all night and a game of
not getting. forgetting. .
losing continues. .
Is there any friend near?
Is there anyone who has a new sky?
From anyone I want to borrow such a sky
where dreams play the magic of the melody
If I get the dear favorable sky, I promise the

door will open and
the light will come
I promise to stand up and fly again
I promise to raise my hand and hold everyone's hand
Now my sky is just filled with darkness
Now just going blind and dying every moment
Now just keeping the face between the knees
Everything is wrong, everything is empty, and everything is just empty!
My sad sky covers my face with that gesture of sadness
My sad sky peeked out of the window of my mind

I am a marginal man

I am a marginal man
I can't think much
All I can think is that
I don't know what to do
I don't know how to do
I don't know if there is anything to do
But I know I have to endure
I know I have to stay
I know I have to carry on
And I have to speak for myself
I am a marginal man
I can't see much
All I can see is a murky sky
The monstrous clouds
A sick sun
The obscure stars
A sobbing moon
And yet, a colourful rainbow !
I am a marginal man
I can't do much
All I can do is to try very hard to touch the rainbow
I must do it because
I must live…

Ashish Kumar Pathak, India

We widows wonder why

Eternal memories flicker
In a far far away sky
I wonder where you gone
Why did you die?
People say time will heal wounds
That can be true
But lonely between times
I start looking for you,
Sitting alone in darkness
And unending despair
Cries my shy lens and tears
My heart is in pieces
Even silence is so deafening
To my awaiting ears,

I wake every morning
As we all do
Trying to reach over for you
You are never there
I remember
What shall I do?
You are gone
Nothing left
But your profound memories
These memories lead me
To utter silence
And tears
I miss your arms
That hold me so tight
Even your defeating snores
Now I miss whole night,
Why the God has taken
You away from me
I am so torn
From my side
Umpteen years we lived
One and so together
I miss you more
When you are out of sight,
Someone please explain me
Why he had to go
Are there any valid reasons
those loving birds

Have rights so right to know?
How lost I am
Without you
There are no words
for me you were world
I wish you knew,
I got up every morning
The sunshine daily
I look into the mirror
I don't find the shine,
I miss your smiling face
That strong strong embrace
It happens so daily
Until I am alive
Is that being the daily case?

Women and we men

What else is as beautiful?
as a woman?
Beautiful inside and out,
when no possessions keep us
man becomes a wanderer but
woman is still a 'wonderess'
in a girl hides a queen
who hides in houses
but dreams for all others,
A woman's happiness
is in throwing everything
to live for love and
prosperity of other,
this beautiful business
of womanhood is a heavy burden
and when a woman says
she is a housewife
she exults in supreme pride
and then aspires no more,
she moves with the grace
with her moves the race
she's is surviving for others,
if you want something said
comes into the picture the man
and if you want something done
there she comes strongly,

she doesn't cook
she burns
for she is a mother,
Wonderful friend, lover
and adviser with smile,.
she is a mystery and delight
the moon that rises within
a woman
doesn't follow and calendar
as the one in the sky
so O man submit yourself
to true friendship
of a woman you love
She heals, encourages and
lifts you higher.

Priyatosh Das, India

God Made The Gigantic Universe. . . .

How artfully the supreme God made the Universe
Made the gigantic world
Made the infinite sky
Made all creature, made all human beings
Made all lifeless things
Of diverse size, shape and colour
And yet the world has beauty of it's own.

God made the earth with enormous diversity
For our *beauteous* life and happiness,
But men divided the world
Based on caste, creed and complexion. . . .
Men divided the world
Based on region, religion and linguistic ethnicity

How foolishly men forget-
The same blood perculates
In our limbs,
in all human beings.
The same air we inhale
To live short span of life

The same love exists in our heart
The same heart melts and bleeds
When profound grief pierces its chambers
Despite thousands of disparities

Life is too short
It is high time to awake and
Fight against all evil and devil
That divides the world with ignorance and narrowness
Based on caste, creed, and complexion based
discrimination.
We must beautify the world
To live a happy and blissful life
N. B Copyright reserved @Priyatosh Das

Let's Take Pledge to Save a Girl

Let's take pledge to save a girl...
save a mother...
and save the human race...
And feel her pains.

Blood what circulates through her veins
Flowing in our head and limbs
Is her blessing in disguise?

She is the queen of beauty
Beauty that fills our heart
With
Boundless charms and love
She is the ocean of eternal love

Forget not how our mother toiled night and day
Forget not how she brought up us with unfathomable love
and care
Excruciating pains were trifling to her
To bloom flourishing smile in our visage

Let's bow down our head to her selfless sacrifice
And save a girl child as the mother race
Love her as the greatest gift
Worship her at the temple of the heart.

She is the most beautiful goddess
Divinely bestowed in the lap of the earth

Partha Banerjee

REMEMBER THOSE

Why so Much deprivation
And Inequality even after
So many years?

And…
How long will they shed tears of violence?

Just to be a woman. . . .
Remember those…
who have eternally made the earth enlighten by giving
birth to holy children for
Centuries…

Remember the achievements of those...
who are on an equal footing with male in all arena of life
Still they received nothing but humiliation
and oppression
Can't we be more humane by going beyond
gender inequality?
Can't we give them back their rights, respect and
empower they deserve?

Sarbashis Kumar Paul

O! My Divine Mother

O! Maa Durga. . .
Confer us blessing
We are worrying.
What's happening?
Having no
Rhythmic explanation
Sometimes seeing it is
Meaningless destruction
Which is seemed to be?
Poetry having no rhythm
And a song having no melody
Nothing happiness and is

Staying in darkness. . .
We want immortal light
Not being interested to fight
Only illumination and illumination
Is our desire of getting perfection?
Bestow me Divine wrath
It's my inner dearth
Only peace is our destination.
Your blessing gives us that realization.

Arbind Kumar Choudhary, India

The Fair Sex

It is the woman
Who fits perfectly?
For free-love
Amidst many a fox-glove
It is the fair sex
Who has remained the star of the screen?
Through thick and thin
Amidst many a goblin
She is the incarnation of the Goddess
Who sets the world on fire?
And sets up shop everywhere
Amidst many a debt of nature
She is the national treasure
Who gives heart failure to the sorry figure?

Woman

It is the woman
Who fights...
Fire with fire
For fair and square
Amidst many a cloud of fire
She barks
But never bites
For the air of sanctity
Amidst many a divinity
It is she
Who puts the saddle on the right horse
Amidst many a play horse
Woman is a master of fate
Who strikes the right note for the Aeolian lute?

Dr. Brajesh Kumar Gupta "Mewadev"

ON THE SURFACE OF THE MIND

Usually, my mind is as big as the universe
Where knowledge is free, minds manufacture miracles
A long embrace that salves a searching mind,
Calling our attention to the mystical lights
Joy is found so tangible here,
Reality is a burden I cannot bear
I can feel the rhythm of my heart
Everyone takes something for granted each and every day
Hoping to grow a brand new miracle
Quite honestly,
It lies to me of what it needs
Flames coming through my eyes
Found only in the heart and the mind
Trying to give our mind and soul
Our timing finally right forever on the mark

Let's try to understand,
I will not stop by my mind maker;
Sharpness of mind creates miracles
Enlightened by crystal chandeliers,
I try to keep running to manufacture miracles from my
mind.
© Dr. Brajesh Kumar Gupta "Mewadev", Banda (U. P. -
India)
@ All Rights Reserved.

LIFE EASIER FOR ME

Hacking and sniffling
I can hear that hacking noise
My hackers poised to do my bidding
Give people things they truly need,
Twisting the law to your greed thus dethroning justice
There is a difference between connoisseurs
Like a cold bitter wind
Sometimes words can be lies liars tell
Hacking, slicing, severing our feelings
And I have to stop breaking words up
The roads are always full of life,
People come and show their means
Here are some more.
@ All Rights Reserved.

214

Sk. Yakubpasha, India

Devil's Monologue

Human no longer to be called human
All they say slowly changing his name as devil of all
His own shadows clearly resemble all his sins
As if in shape of Devil's horns and sharp teeth.
All species were born to live freely
But man vanishing them slowly.
Here the conflict not only between man and beasts
But also between he and she.
His lustful desire can kill her burying as well
Though, they say devil is lurking in all his deeds.
Yes, I dwell in filthy hearts as noble art
I follow him like a lurking shadow
When man about to do heinous act.
Then I give my evil grin and fly on invisible shallows.
But, I do not claim that was my diabolic crime
Here man is making hellish things on earth.

I stood beside when he cut her flesh
Into pieces, oh! My goodness
When I was called the reason of all
Since then started ill angels fall
Once I provoked you to douse my jealous
But not for mere pleasure or evil's treasure.
Oh! Man now I am afraid to see you
Your sins doubled and tripled
And your shadows turned into giant
gargoyle winged shapes.
Oh! Man decide who won this land of God
Either you or me, who knows than me (he faded away with
evil grin

I Woke Up in My Dream

Birth and death are mystery
between these two is my life journey
Amazingly heart connected this, with
Sensitive tone of beat until my last breath
My birth and life is not for long
However, trees and creepers are somehow strong
I feel alone and wanted to be alone
When I was poorly treated by others as clown
It witched and jittered in anxiety to achieve endless goal
Lost of interest and tiredness as if evermore
One night in unsteady feeble light
My mind tempted me to suicide
With consumed poison of depression, I slept.
Everything was dark inside my heart.
But a sliver of light fell and grew slowly
When someone opened windows door.
A caterpillar slouching towards windows pane
Though nothing was there it moved in hasty-catchy way.
Out of nowhere appeared Devine's hand
wonderfully caterpillar turned into colourful butterfly.
Finally flashed a hope of life inside deep
As butterfly emerged out of divine light.
Then I realized and woke up in my dream
No creature attain freedom with answer of death.

Jupinderjit Singh, India

Rape of a flower

My fragrance had no parallel…
beauty sublime
Petals soft and shy…
and colourful than the most beautiful butterfly

other flowers were around…
none matched my youth on that ground
Darling I was of all
Among young, old, big or small…

Drones and bees tried their best
To come near, taste my honey
but failed the test
I had a prince in my heart
who would complete
my incomplete part

Then an ugly hand hovered on
Plucked me apart with one stroke
I could not even cry or mourn

An ugly iron pin tore into me
I was hung on the man›s stage
with other flowers like me separated from this

beautiful land
They called it a victory garland
Where music happened
And dramas were played
Muted I cried
but no one could see...

I bled and struggled for breath
They whistled and clapped

much before their show was over
I bled and dried up there, dead, ugly
a victim of the mighty and their greed

not even a single drop left
to bleed.... .

Krishnasankar Acharjee

TRANSGENDER

But love transgender's tourney, non-stop
In that bottom the social sensations flop.

They break the neolithic-natures, smiling.
Make untrue, the unjust youth perceiving

With due connection they daub daylights.
In a contrary as third gender, who plights.

Of lithe-likings, the stars smile with jovial.
Think later they love each-other bisexual.

Bears, transgender-taint from successor
On theoretic voids all owning as warrior

Into their esse-awaked-visions, intangible
From era, the attained youth never livable

Now, to lay the veil true men join by them.
And gets Real River's resort, touching-gem

Near to neighbour with affectionate love.
As stream their softy sound, swell above.

Into the object they tired, fossilized slave
Within a solemn vow sweaty soma, rave

From slippy slopes poet finds roses-rear.
Their sleepless souls sigh, upon the year

In their pith colourless love feelings pain
Thro, the city's news poet alarming again.

To hope ensuing existence, they abiding
Lastly as the sun-shine, leap for enjoying.

Binay Laha

Before me

Many questions are kept before me as I am a woman.
I can't get up late.
I can't sleep late.
I am a woman.

I can't stay all alone.
I can't move freely in the streets late at night.

If I smoke I am a characterless.
If I break the tie I am a characterless.
But I am blessed to be a woman for I give birth to the
world, solemnly

Marginal

The morning chant is over
The temple is closed
Here is a man who was sweeping the floor
People call him untouchable...

Neither is he allowed to pray
Nor is he allowed to enter the temple
He is serving the humanity ages after ages and dying
As a Untouchable dies...

Dr. Ratan Ghosh, India

SECONDARY BEING

Being the Secondary being…
Once I had to sing with pseudonym
In this world of so-called human and men

Perhaps the justice denied by the morn
When a piece of flesh was torn
Only to make me a marginalized born

Perhaps the wonder was for the first Man!
Why was this different clan?
'Is this a God's plan'?

The wonder fruit that was whimsically plucked
Only to stigmatize my helpless luck

In the garden of dishonor and fuck

Centuries and Centuries gone...
Sometimes as better half and sometimes as porn
In this land of lovelorn...

As a civilized porn
Where minds, hearts, souls and breasts secondly torn
Sometimes as lovelorn and sometimes as porn

In a land of lovelorn
Where men, beasts and demons are equally born ...
Only to seduce His virgin daughters and Moms
Only to seduce His virgin daughters and Moms
Dr. Ratan Ghosh©®

SECONDARY CLAN

Scanned. . .
It seems as if I am not of a same clan
In the bed of men and women
Since I feel the beatings of my heart
I find the X-rays begin touching my sensitive parts
In a land of lust and lost love
If by chance I get a space to wink
I know I will be dragged down slowly to sink…
In the bed of pale and pink!
My morning often finds the walking dark clouds
Seizing and knocking me to drop down as piece of clods
Seizing and knocking me to drop down as piece of clods
In a land of man-made huts
In a land of man-made huts
Dr. Ratan Ghosh©®

WITHERING BUDS

I see the withering buds. . .
Being thrown away and heaped up in the nameless
dustbins and guts
Perhaps they had a solemn prayer for the morning ray
While slowly growing up in the bed of the same clay
Rolling and rolling round for a few seasonal weeks
Never could they feel the earthly tricks. . .
Suddenly a mortal storm knocking the veins
Ultrasound and Anomaly scan threatening all the strengths
The shining swords walking ahead to chop off their breaths
Secretly falling down by the nameless streets...
My heart pines seeing these secret shameless games
Where all are born from the same passionate flames
Hearts killing the hearts in such nameless civilized earth
Who knows one day my earth may die in the
dustbins of birth!
No no no no more the earth one day will be able to pine
When men and women will slowly forget to sing
the spring-time rhyme
Dr. Ratan Ghosh©®

OUR EARTH

Tongues gone...
Voices gone...
And gone thereby the fainted breasts

Lips gone...
Passions gone...
And gone thereby all the rests

Hopes gone...
Homes gone...
And gone thereby all the known streets

Chaste gone...
Names gone...
And gone thereby all our greets
Since our souls lost in the bed of helpless needs

Mornings gone...
Nights gone ...
And gone all things good and bad

We are not human beings but beasts instead
Born to taste only the lusty semen and breads
Born to taste only the lusty semen and breads

In our nameless earthly nests
In our nameless earthly nests

Where Oedipus is born to violate mother's breasts
Where Oedipus is born to violate mother's breasts
Dr. Ratan Ghosh©®

WE ARE NOT HUMAN BUT GAY MEN

Being a different being
Never do we see the beauty of lively 'Spring'
In the stigmatized room of our earthly beings

Walking by the fainted streets and lanes...
We see the engraved stories of our pains
Though we know, no dictionary can explain...
The stresses and strains...

Where we are living without love, blessings and passionate
drops of rain?
In the world of men and women
In the world of men and women

The dawn, morning and the night
Never have they smelled our infertile land alike
Never have they smelled our infertile land alike

Often do we die?
By the flood of tears and sigh
Only to say to this unaccustomed earth bye bye
Dr. Ratan Ghosh©®

AUTHORS

Sonjayemaurya, Artist, Mumbai

Sonjaye Maurya is an eminent artist with international recognition. He is a self taught artist who has made a strong niche in the world of art in a short span. He is bestowed with numerous awards like 'KalaRatn', 'Swami Vivekananda Excellence Award', and Honorary Doctorate to name a few. He is also a 'World Peace &Brotherhood' and 'World Humanity Ambassador' His works have a mysterious quality. . . a magical touch that makes them stand apart from the work so for the contemporary artists. Everything that he paints has a deep meaning and message in it. May it be Buddha or even if he is painting fishes or a landscape. His works are many a times a transformation from realistic to abstract and vice versa.

Lucilla Trapazzo

Lucilla Trapazzo has studied German Literature (Rome, Italy), Film-Video (Washington, D. C.), and theater. She is a Poetry editor of "Mockup Magazine", Italy, a member of art and literature associations internationally. Her literary and cultural activities rest on poetry, theatre, installations, translations, juror/moderator of International poetry festivals and literary critiques. Her poems have been translated in ten languages and awarded numerous prizes. Her poems are published in International anthologies and magazines.

Joanna Svensson

Joanna Svensson, a Swedish writer, poet and novelist since early teens. She has Published 8 books of poetry in English, Swedish, Polish and German and 3 fiction novels. She participates in several international anthologies. She is a Member of Swedish Author Association. She was Awarded 1st prize in prose in Bucharest 2019. She participates in literary festivals around the world.

Jana Orlov

Jana Orlová (1986) is a Czech poet and a performer. She published „Sniff the Fire" in 2012 and "Újedě" in 2017, and books in Ukrainian and Romanian in 2019. Her poems were translated into Hindi, English, Chinese, Spanish, Arabic, Belarusian, Polish, Bulgarian, Greek and Italian. Her work is to be seen at www. janaorlova. cz.

Alicia Minjarez Ramírez, MEXICO

She is an internationally renowned Mexican poetess and author who has won numerous awards including: the Excellence Prize World Poetry Championship Romania 2019. Literary Prize "Tra le Parole e L'infinito" Italy 2019. EASAL medal Award by the European Academy of Sciences and Letters France 2018

Kapardeli Eftichia Greece-Patra

She has a Doctorate from ARTS AND CULTURE WORLD ACADEMY. She lives in Patras. She writes poetry, stories, short stories, haiku, essays. She has studied journalism from A. K. E. M. and has many awards in national competitions. She has many national and international anthologies to her credit. She is a member of the World Poets' society **of the IWA**, IWA Certify 2017 as the best translation and **member** of the **POETAS DEL MUNDO**.

Paula Louise Shene

Paula Louise Shene, a U. S based multi-genre writer, a college administrator and a business owner is known for her Children's stories, Science-fiction and Fantasy stories. She is also known for her articles on lifestyle, psychology and health. She writes poetry on Free Style, Acrostic, and Rhyme. She is an illustrators, editor and avid researcher in her quest for eclectic knowledge.

Miljana Zivanovic

Miljana Zivanovic was born in Vukovar, Croatia. She lives and writes in Switzerland. "A Walk in the Saffron Valley" is her first independent edition of poetry. She participates in eight Anthologies. Out of 1567 writers of the Free Artists of Autrsalia, 30 best authors were chosen,

Miljana Živanović is one of the selected best writers for 2019. The first prize at the literary event "Gordana Koceva 2020" Macedonia and the first prize for the Lyrical Poetry of Macedonia.

Ngozi Olivia Osuoha

Ngozi Olivia Osuoha is a Nigerian poet/writer/thinker/author. She's a graduate of Estate Management with experience in Banking and Broadcasting. She has featured in over sixty international anthologies and has equally published over two hundred and sixty poems in over twenty five countries. She has authored twenty three poetry books and some of them are archived in the United States' Library of Congress. She is also a tailor. Some of her poems have been nominated for both the **Best of the Net Awards** and **Pushcart Prize**. Some of her works have also been translated into and published in some languages, including Spanish, Arabic, Farsi, Macedonian, Russian, Romanian, Khloe, Polish, among others.

Eliza Segiet

Eliza Segiet graduated with a Master's Degree in Philosophy, Arts and Literature at Jagiellonian University. Author's poems Questions and Sea of Mists won the title of the International Publication of the Year 2017 and 2018 in Spillwords Press. She was nominated for the Pushcart

Prize in 2019 and for the iWoman Global Awards. She was awarded Laureate NajiNaaman Literary Prize 2020 and Laureate International Award Paragon of Hope (2020).

Monica Maartens, South African

Zararia Yul is a pen name, meaning rising of Dawn River beyond the horizon. . . . a South African born poetess and author with ten published books. She shares her experiences, her darkness and light, her falls and rises with her readers in the hope of shedding some precious light into all the pitfalls and troubles life has to offer. . . . making for very interesting and thought provoking reading. Do enjoy. . .

Jialing Huis

Jialing Huis from Mainland China and lives in Hong Kong for 5 years now. She believes that uncertainties in the future are also nested with possibilities, if we cooperate. She loves reading, writing, cooking, appreciating arts and walking in the nature. She aspires to be a voice for the voiceless.

Sue Zhu (淑文)

Sue Zhu (淑文), New Zealand Chinese poet, Artist, organizer of international cultural exchange used to be the TV presenter in China is a member of Chinese Poetry Society, director of NZ Poem Art Association, honorary director of the US-China Cultural Association, One of the founders of "All Souls Poetry" club, an Editor and advisor for more than 20 Chinese poetry clubs and magazines in China, USA and NZ. She has won the IL Meleto di Guido Gozzano Literary Prize (International Section) – X (2020) in 2020. Pushcart Prize Nomination (USA) in 2020. Year 2019 she was awarded the certificate of Munir Mezyed Foundation for Arts and Culture.

Dr. Tarana Turan Rahimli

Dr. Tarana Turan Rahimli is an Azerbaijani poet, writer, journalist, translator, literary critic, academic, is an active member of the International Literary Agency in Turkey and Azerbaijan. She is a PhD in Philology, Associate Professor of Azerbaijan and World Literature Chair of Azerbaijan State Pedagogical University, author of 7 books and more than 400 articles. The work has been published in more than 25 Western and Eastern countries.

Selma Kopić

Selma Kopić, professor, born in 1962 in Tuzla, Bosnia and Herzegovina. Her stories and poems have entered anthologies around the world. The most significant is the third prize "Mak Dizdar", Stolac, BiH, 2008 for the unpublished collection of poems "Puzzle". She has published two collections of poems: 'The Sign' Print Com Tuzla and 'The Monument of Love' Poetry Planet Publishing House.

Tali Cohen Shabtai

Tali Cohen Shabtai, is a poet, she was born in Jerusalem, Israel. She began writing poetry at the age of six, Tali's poems expresses spiritual and physical exile. She is studying her exile and freedom paradox, her cosmopolitan vision is very obvious in her writings. She lived some years in Oslo Norway and in the U. S. A. Tali has written three poetry books:" *"Purple Diluted in a Black's Thick"*, (bilingual 2007), "Protest" (bilingual 2012) and *"Nine Years From You"* (2018).

By 2021, her fourth book of poetry will be published which will also be published in Norway. Her literary works have been translated and published into many languages as well.

Dr. Meenakshi Mohan

Dr. Meenakshi Mohan is a scholar, writer, and artist. She has taught at universities in Chicago, Boston, and Towson University in Maryland. She is on the Editorial Team for *Inquiry in Education*, a peer-reviewed journal published by National Louis University, Chicago, Illinois. Meenakshi lives in Maryland, USA.

Jyotirmaya Thakur

Jyotirmaya Thakur is a retired principal, author of thirty books with many waiting to be published and translated in 38 languages in International anthologies in many countries. She is a Hindi translator in ITHACA magazine of Spain. She is a Multi-Genre Award Winner, Reviewer, Columnist, Editor, academician, motivational speaker, a philanthropist, spiritual and a social activist and a true scholar. She is an internationally renowned poet and writer, who has won numerous awards, for both her literature and humanitarian efforts. She exemplifies the ideal that writing is more than just words on paper; it is a means of creating positive change in the world.

Roopali Sircar Gaur, Ph. D.

Roopali Sircar Gaur, Ph. D. is a lifelong teacher, poet-performer, writer, environmentalist, and social justice activist. Roopali retired as

Associate Professor of English from Delhi University. She is a widely published columnist and writer, who has written for peer-reviewed journals, and served on academic conference panels worldwide.

Dr. Chanchal Sarin

Dr. Chanchal Sarin, retired Associate Professor, University of Delhi, lives in Gurgaon, India. She authored seven books on Genetics and Biology besides several articles on research and popular science. She contributed to many poetry forums. She has always endeavored to create interest among students and young generations to serve community with the aim to eliminate ignorance and increase scientific temperament.

Pankhuri Sinha

Pankhuri Sinha is a bilingual young poet and story writer from India, who has lived in North America for 14 years. Two books of poems published in English, two collections of stories published in Hindi, five collections of poetries published in Hindi, and many more are lined up. Has won many prestigious, national-international awards, has been translated in over twenty one languages. Her writing is dominated by themes of exile and immigration, gender equality and environmental concerns.

Niharika Chibber Joe

Niharika Chibber Joe is a U. S. civil servant. She is also a published poet and short story writer. Most recently, her work has been published in *In All the Spaces: Diverse Voices in Global Women's Poetry* (2020), *Millennium Poesy* (2021), *Earth, Fire, Water, Wind* (2021) and in the *Setu Online Literary Journal*. She holds degrees in Japanese from the Jawaharlal Nehru University, and an M. A. from the Johns Hopkins University's School of Advanced International Studies in Washington, D. C.

Sarita Naik

Sarita Naik works as a lecturer in English at Pipli College, Puri, hailing from Sonepur, Odisha. She is a passionate poet from India. Her passion includes composing poems, writing essays and articles. She has received Gold Medal in M. Phil English from Gangadhar Meher University, India. She has written a lot of poems and her poems deal with the variety of subjects like love, peace, gender discrimination, violence. She is an advocate and representative of her own gender. Her poem 'Woman' has been published in Replica. She often writes about the true importance and significance of women and on their role in history. Her poem 'Being a Girl' is published in Vasudha. She is an internationally acclaimed author and has been appreciated by the national and international literary circles.

Jyoti Sahni

Jyoti Sahni has published two books in Hindi poetry: "Tanisha" & "Chetna". All the proceeds from the sales of both the books were given to Lions Club International Foundation for diabetes and childhood cancer research. She lives with her two kids and husband in New Jersey USA.

Padmaja Iyengar-Paddy's

Padmaja Iyengar-Paddy's maiden poetry collection 'P-En-Chants' has been recognized by the India Book of Records. A recipient of several awards, Paddy has compiled and edited 6 international multilingual poetry anthologies 'Amaravati Poetic Prism' 2016 to 2019, recognized by Coca-Cola India's Limca Book of Records as "Poetry Anthology in Most Languages".

Sriparna Bandyopadhyay

Sriparna Bandyopadhyay, has eleven published books of poetry, juvenile fictions, micro stories, short stories, essay, features, comedy fictions in her credit and some more are in queue. Recognition received so far are 'Bango Samskriti Samman, 2012, 'Rritobak' short story competition 2016, Sharmila Ghosh Sahitya Puraskar 2016, Usha Bhattacharya Smriti Sahitya Puraskar 2018, Nabaprabhat Rajat Jayanti Barsha Sammanana

2018, Pratilipi Special Award (short story) 2020, Pratilipi First Prize (Novella) 2020, Rajesh Sarkar Smriti Puraskar, 2020.

Snigdha Agrawal

Snigdha Agrawal writes all genres of poetry, prose, short stories, travel diaries. Educated in Loreto Institutions, and brought up in a cosmopolitan environment, she has learnt the best of the east and west. She is a published author of two books of poems "EVOCATIVE RENDERINGS" and "TALES OF THE TWINS unsung melodies", apart from contributions to several published anthologies.

Sasha Banhotra

Sasha Banhotra is a writer, a poet, and a teacher. Born in Jammu and currently settled in Delhi, she has been writing articles and poems about social issues in the education sector in various newspapers and magazines of J&K, India. Her poems can be found in globally published Anthologies.

Hema Ravi

Hema Ravi, freelance trainer for IELTS and Communicative English, is a poet, author, reviewer, independent researcher, event organizer and editor of Efflorescence (published by the Chennai Poets' Circle). Her verses and write ups have been featured in several online and international print journals; she is among the 'Distinguished Writers 2021, ' having won the ninth place in the 7th Bharat Award for Literature International Short Story Contest.

Meher Pestonji

Meher Pestonji has been a journalist for over 30 years. Her two novels 'Pervez' and 'Sadak Chhaap' are based on her experiences as journalist. Her poems reflect a deep connection with Nature and also talk of resilience as a survival tool

Renette Peterson D'Souza

Renette Peterson D'Souza - writer and editor, is an economics post graduate from Mumbai-India. She is also an entrepreneur and social activist for empowerment of women from Mumbai and is a strong believer in the simple policy of 'Live and let live'. With a zest for life and a penchant for writing poetry, she has penned many poems on a broad range of topics through social media and many online worldwide poetry forums and E magazines. Her poems have been read on International platforms and have been published in various National as well as International anthologies

Sutanuka Mondal

Sutanuka Mondal is from Durgapur, a city in West Bengal. Having finished her M. A. in English and Culture Studies, she is now pursuing Bed. An avid reader, a budding writer and poet she also enjoys listening to music, her poems got featured in *Afrobizgermany* and The Indian Rover web magazine

Mrs Namita Rani Panda

Mrs Namita Rani Panda is a multilingual poet, story writer and translator from Sambalpur of Odisha, India. She now works as Vice-Principal of Jawahar Navodaya Vidyalaya, Cuttack under the Ministry of HRD, Dept. of School Education and Literacy, Govt. of India. She has five anthologies of poems to her credit: Blue Butterflies, Rippling Feelings, A Slice of Sky and A Song for Myself and Colours of Love. She has co-authored Rivulets of Reflections, a book of translated stories. Her signature words are love, optimism and self-confidence. She is an active member of Cosmic Crew, a literary group of women poets in Odisha working with the motto "My pen for the world. " She is editor of Radical Rhythm-2, an anthology of poems by Cosmic Crew.

Satabdi Saha

Satabdi Saha is an ex- professor, a bilingual poet and author. Her English Publications in print are as follows:
1. Prose and poetry in various journals, including that of Calcutta University **2.** 2010- A book of poems titled, BLOOD, DREAMS AND PAIN, publisher, Writers Workshop **3.** 2014- A collection of poems and short stories titled OF HAWKS AND SPARROWS, Patridge Publications. **4.** Publications of stories, essays and autobiography in 5 anthologies by Sweetycat Press. **5.** Poem selected for online publication by Clarendon House Publication and also in the upcoming printed anthology. **6.** Various national and international online magazines

Misna Chanu

She contributed her poetry in many Anthologies and published a poetry book entitled *"A Little Piece Of Melancholic Sky"*. Her second Book, an international bilingual anthology *"Under The Azure Sky'* is under publication.

Namramita Banerjee

Namramita Banerjee is a passionate writer for 9 years. Her works have been published in National and International magazines, newspapers as well as on quite a few online websites and blogs. Presently she is working in Bollywood as a screenplay writer for the past two years. Having a Master's degree in English and Psychology, she is quite good at understanding the psychology of people. She is a voracious reader and a logophile. She loves to unleash her inner conflict through writing. She is a bong girl, a solitude lover, a foodie, and a globe-trotter.

Srutakirti Tripathy

A passionate writer from Odisha writing poems, stories both in English and odia language since 3 years. Few of them got published in newspaper, magazines. .

Sonia Ghosh

Sonia Ghosh is from Hooghly in West Bengal. After finishing her M. A in English literature she is pursuing Bed from Beta College Of Education under University Of Burdwan. She enjoys reading poetry, story books and colours her imaginations through pen.

Boby Borah

Boby Borah is a notable writer of Assam, India. She has composed two of her assortments of verse specifically" Dohut Khamusi" and "Anubhobe Sui Juwer Porot" and she is also a sensitive columnist of Assam. She completed her masters in Assamese language from Guwahati University. She is presently the President of *Doomdoma Women Organisation* and the founder of *Sankardev Shisu Niketan*. She was awarded *"Virangana Savitri Bai Phule Fellowship* by Bhartiya Dalit Sahitya Akademi, Delhi and *Sanker Aazan Samanboi Award*-2019 by *Sahitya Samaj Sanskritik Seva Manch* (Assam).

Dr. Megha Bharati 'Meghall'

Dr. Megha Bharati 'Meghall', better known as the "Queen of Kumaun", is a Poet, Author, Singer, Lyricist, Professor, Academic & a Social Activist with three Books & Several Film's and Music Album's to her credit. As a Singer & Lyricist her songs are a craze in countries other than India too. As an Author and Poet her books have hailed Five Star ratings in the US. She writes in distinct languages such as English, Hindi, Urdu and Kumaoni and has been honoured with several Awards, Recognitions and Titles for the same. {meghabharati777@yahoo. in}

Kanta Roy, (India)

Kanta Roy, (India) a poetess and painter and a retired Government Teacher, bilingual poetess, writing as passion and hobby, she believes poetry and paintings are correlated with spreads, main passion on abstract paintings so like poems are metaphorical. Her special choice is structured poetry in her own dilute. So many poems are awarded for excellence and published in anthologies

Sujata Paul

Sujata Paul is a bilingual poetess. By profession she is a teacher but writing is her passion. She loves travelling, music and a nature lover. She has published three poetry books, "WHISPER OF MY SOUL" and "SARANG" in English and "ASTITWA" in Bengali. . Her poetries, articles and prose have been published in different national and international journals and anthologies. Her articles and poem on Colour Based Discrimination received Double Cross Medal from Italy and South Africa. She is a regular contributor of different National and International E Magazines. Her creative writings are witnessed by the special anthologies like "Tranquil Muse", International Anthology of Poems on "Autism", "Spilling Essences", "Vasudha", "Scintillating Scions", "Queen", "The Spirit of India", "SIPAY", and another international Anthology and so on. She has been awarded Sahitya Academy Award by Gujrat Sahitya Academy in 2020. She has also been awarded Nari Samman by Literoma and The Most Influential Women Award by The Spirit Mania. She is also the recipient of Literary Excellence Award by Suryodaya Literary Foundation, Odisha in 2020. She is the founder of Creative Tripura, a wonderful Poetry group.

Deepti mohapatra

Deepti mohapatra is from Odisha while currently residing in Punjab, a homemaker with very much passionate in writing. She has contributed her poems and stories in different Anthologies. She loves writing poems, stories, blogs and quotes.

Hussein Habasch

Hussein Habasch is a poet from Afrin, Kurdistan. His poems have been translated into many languages. He participated in many international festivals of poetry including: Colombia, Nicaragua, France, Puerto Rico, Mexico, Germany, Romania, Lithuania, Morocco, Ecuador, El Salvador, Kosovo, Macedonia, Costa Rica, Slovenia, China, Taiwan and New York City.

Mgr. Mircea Dan Duta

Assoc. Prof. Mgr. Mircea Dan Duta, (PhD.) is a faculty of Social Sciences, Charles University, Prague Poet, translator, film scientist, Editor, Poet, Film scientist, Translator and author of Czech expression. He is the Editor of **Levure Littéraire** (France – USA-Germany), **FITRALIT** (Romania), **A Too Powerful Word (**Serbia), **Quest** (Montenegro), producer &moderator of cultural events in the Czech Republic, Slovak Republic and Romania. **His Poetry books are- Landscapes, Flights and Dictations, Tin quotes, inferiority complexes and human rights** (2014/2015, **Petr Štengl Editions**, Prague), **Plíz sujčov jor mobajl foun senťu / Pliiz suiciof ior mobail faun senchiu** (Next Page Editions, Bucharest, 2020, bilingual Czech-Romanian anthology). Samples from his scientific work are– (film and literary critic and history): Narrator, Author & God (Charles University Press, 2009), The Holocaust in the Czech, Slovak and Polish Literature & Cinema (ibid. , 2007), The Czech & Slovak Film New Wave in the Social, Political and Cultural Contextof the 60s of the 20th Century (**Jozef Škvorecký** Literary Academy Press, 2008) – last two titles are collective works.

Translator: Czech/Slovak < – >Romanian;

Polish, Bulgarian -> Romanian

English, French < – >Romanian

Parts of his work were translated and published in the USA, France, United Kingdom, Spain, Poland, Bulgaria, Israel, Serbia, Romania, Moldavia, Montenegro, North Macedonia, Spain, India, Egipt, Syria, Korea, Albania, Kossovo, Mongolia. He is also present in anthologies in the USA, UK, Mongolia, Spain, South-Africa, India, Indonesia, Romania, and Moldavia.

Maid Corbic

Maid Corbic comes from Bosnia and Herzegovina. He has twenty one years, and lives in Tuzla. He spends most of his free time writing and reading books. His works have been published in numerous portals such as:„Kosovo Peonies", „Amritanyali Journal", „Krajberzje. mk", „VIS Internationally Magazine" and many others.

Isaac Cohen

Isaac Cohen published a book, *The Moment of Silence*, in 1983. He has done work as a writer of prose and poetry, translator, artist and painter. His writings in Hebrew were published in an anthology at "Eiton 77", and in their literary periodical. Other literary periodicals who published his works included "Apirion", "Dimui", "Mabua" and "Mahut. " He has studied with leading Israeli Novelists such as Amos Oz, Yehuda Amichai and Dan Tzalka. Prizes he won include, "Free Masons prize for writing", 1996. An honorable mentionat "The Miriam Lindberg, Competition for Peace" and The "Mifal Hapais Prize for Poetry", in 2002. He was the manager of the Logic Puzzles Club for"Motke" website. He is theauthor of several new Herschelle jokes. (Herschelle is an Eastern European comic figure and the subject of jokes and humorous folk-tales). His poems were translated to Spanish, Russian, Tamil and Philippine. He is a veteran member of Voices Israel – a group of poets writing in English. Their Newsletter has published many poems of his over the years. The anthologies "ATUNIS" (2019), "Voices"(1999, 2000) and "Determinations2" (1997) contain poems of his. He is active in Israel's cultural life.

Fareed Agyakwah

Fareed Agyakwah is a prolific African writer. On International Women's Day in 2019, from Literature Lover's Association, Agyakwah received a Bronze Star Award for his poetry. Agyakwah is also a recipient of Termirqazyq Best Poet/ Writer of the World 2019. He is the author of *A Child's Poetry for Peace*.

MONSIF BEROUAL

MONSIF BEROUAL is an International renowned poet from Morocco. He has received multiple awards, including: The World Icon of Literature of the National Academy of Arts and Culture, (India, 2020) and The Pablo Neruda Medal (2017). He is the Youth Ambassador of Morocco for Inner Child Press International.

Dr. K. V. DOMINIC,

Dr. K. V. DOMINIC, English poet, short story writer, critic and editor is a retired Associate Professor of the Post Graduate & Research Department of English, Newman College, Thodupuzha, Kerala, India. He has authored/edited 41 books including seven collections of poems and two short story books. He is the Secretary of GIEWEC, Editor of WEC and IJML.

Alan Cherian Puthenpurayil

Alan Cherian Puthenpurayil (ACP) is a bilingual poet and critic from India who has notched up a significant place in the literary field Pedigree. Through his simple style, profound thematic presentations, aesthetic writings, creative endeavors, calm and quiet attitude, supple wavelength of the heart, regenerative mentality, preserving mindset, exploration of manifold themes with easiness, academic credentials, commitment to social causes, solidarity with the poor and the downtrodden, hundred percentage devotion to the tasks at hand and enormous dedication to poetic vibrancies, he has notched up a vital place in the world of poetry today.

Khesise lungma

Khesise lungma is poet from Bhutan, he is self-employed. So far he has written more than thousand poems and most of his poems are published in Bharat visions websites. Kishor Mongar is his original name and he hails from Gelephu town located Sarpang Bhutan.

MD AHTESHAM AHMAD:

MD AHTESHAM AHMAD: An educator, author and a journalist and poet, **MD AHTESHAM AHMAD** hailing from a small town called ANDAL in WEST BENGAL writes multilingual in English, Hinglish, Hindi, Urdu and sometimes in Bengali in various genres for newspapers and journals of national and international repute. Many a composition penned by him has been published at home and abroad.

Tapankanti Mukherjee

An M. A in English from Calcutta University he is a Retired Bank Officer. He writes poems, short - stories, essays in the literary magazines of India, Canada, Bangladesh, Germany. Published books - *Hridaypurer Padyakatha* and *Kabitar Kachakachi*. He has Visited Bangladesh five times on ' sahitya safar '

Bagawath Bhandari

Bagawath Bhandari is a teacher by profession and a poet by passion. He has published one of his anthologies titled "Poems with No Rhymes or Reasons" and he is in verge of publishing one more anthology titled "The Thirty Shade of Life. " He has written over 1200 poems and won international awards and recognitions in the field of literature. He started penning a few of his poems when he was a student and got drenched in the Poetry thereafter. Writing became his leisure pursuit and kept on penning down his feelings in everyday's life. To transcend in the field of literature his poems are published in an international anthologies like "A Spark of Hope II", "The Circle of Life", "Florets of Fancy", "Break the Silence", "The Creation Times I", "The Creation Times II", "A Bowl of Peace" "The Wings Volume III", "The Pillar", "Rhadephoresis" "Seeking Human Kindness" and "Scents" Some of his best poems are translated in Nepali, Spanish, Dzongkha and Dari and are published for positive purposes. He is the possessor of ten anthologies, one novel and two stories which are in the threshold of publication. Writing became a food for his soul to feed on.

Dr. Shubhashish Banerjee

Dr. Shubhashish Banerjee is a lecturer of English by profession and holds a doctoral degree of specialization on Tagore's poetry. He has been teaching English in varied fields since 1999 and has composed innumerable poems in English, Hindi and Bengali dealing with the problems of life, human emotions, spirituality and mysticism. He also nurtures flair for journalism and has several articles published to his credit in national dailies. As a teacher, he intends to bring about a radical transformation in human cognizance and perception by portraying the reality in subtle rhyme emanating from the heart in terms of quintessential melody.

Sankha Ranjan Patra

The poet belongs to West Bengal, India. He was born in 1991. His parents are Mr. Santosh Patra and Mrs Chhaya Patra. He is a bilingual poet. He writes in English and Bengali. Besides, he is interested in short story writing. His poems have been published in several anthologies. His published book is *Muse, a collection of poems*.

Orbindu Ganga:

Orbindu Ganga: is an Indian science post-graduate and the first recipient of Dr Mitra Augustine gold medal for academic excellence. He is the founding director of English Literary Journal INNSÆI, author, poet, content writer, painter, researcher, and spiritual healer. He has published many poems, research papers, articles, and a painting.

Ayodhyanath Choudhary,

Ayodhyanath Choudhary, an M. A. In English, has been writing in English and getting published since 1968. His short story "Sympathy", first of all, was published in the illustrated college magazine "Videh "of C. M. College, Darbhanga of the then Bihar University. Though interested in different genres of literature, his passion for writing poetry is great, and he looks forward to getting an anthology of poetry published shortly.

Abhijit Chakraborty

Abhijit Chakraborty is a poet from West Bengal. India. He loves poetry, prose, music etc. He writes in his mother tongue Bengali and in English language. Some poems written (in Bengali and in English) by him were published in some national and international anthologies and literary magazines. A collection of his Bengali poems has been published in Kolkata International Book Fair-2020.

Ashish Kumar Pathak

Ashish Kumar Pathak is a middle school teacher posted at Dharhara block in Munger district of bihar province (India). He has got a letter of appreciation from the president of India for his poem; he is slated to be featured in the mahatma Gandhi anthology which will be released in September 2019. Along with other poets and writers he has been conferred world union of poets Gold cross medal for his contribution in the world book 'Complexion based discrimination. He is the member of the global literati Council under the soothing Prof Deen Dayal. He is only one of the six poets from Asia to be second consecutive year in the Marula world anthology under world renowned Michel Ellis. He has been associated with Glomag, Sahitya Anand and impressive. Recently he has been shortlisted for doctor of letters from writers capital Italy.

Priyatosh Das

Priyatosh Das is a poet of eminent pedigree; he is a bilingual poet, writer, blogger, thinker, story writer, critic, researcher, peace activist and Philanthropist hailing from the Indian state of Assam. He has been practicing literature for the last two and half decade. He is a member of the World UNION OF POETS (Italy), WORLD POETS SOCIETY, LARRISSA(GREEC), INTERNATIONAL WRITERS' ASSOCIATION(BELGIUM)WORLD HIGHER LITERARY ACADEMIC COUNCIL OF WORLD NATIONS WRITERS UNION OF KAZHAKHSTAN. He is the SPECIAL ADVISOR for India for art and culture of the WORLD ACADEMY OF LITERATURE, HISTORY, ART AND CULTURE (MEXICO) He has been honored with MASTER IN CREATIVE WRITING, DOCTORATE IN LITERATURE (Honoris Causa) by the The Latin American Academy Of Modern Literature, MEXICO, DOCTORATE IN LITERATURE, DOCTORATE IN EDUCATION, DOCTORATE IN HUMANITIES Honoris Causa from SERBIA. Besides, he was also conferred upon 'Mahatma Gandhi Peace Award', 'INTERNATIONAL ICON OF LITERATURE AWARD', INTERNATIONAL HUMANITY AWARD›, ›NHRF LITERARY

AWARD 2019› ‹World Icon Of Peace Award'. He was honoured with the ‹World Icon Of Literature ‹World Laureate Of Poetry ‹ by the Latin Academy of Modern Literature, MEXICO. World Icon of Literature award by the Global Academy Of Health, Human Rights and Peace, India.

Partha Banerjee

He is a bi-lingual poet, short story writer and musician. He is the editor of 'Mirror of Time', the leading bi-lingual (English-Bengali) journal of West Bengal. He has received many awards for his contribution in contemporary Bengali literature

Sarbashis Kumar Paul

Sarbashis Kumar Paul is an author, editor, teacher, and organizer. His editorials, book reviews, and writing on various issues have been published in Indian's leading newspapers and magazines. His poems and articles have been published in many national and international books. He is an author of anthologies in English entitled " Gravity: A collection of poems ", " Immortal Imagination " anthology in Bengali " Sasim Theke Asime". He has compiled and edited international anthologies entitled "Versatile Verses ", Heart of Lightness, and "New Dawn" and an anthology in Bengali "Alor Pathe". He has compiled and edited international books of articles entitled " Peace: A pathway to love and

Harmony "and "Trajectory: A global voice of Science and Literature", Apart from that, he has successfully organized the International literary festival and International seminar on peace. He passed B. sc in Mathematics (Hons).

Dr. Brajesh Kumar Gupta

Dr. Brajesh Kumar Gupta "Mewadev" is a recipient of the Presidency of the International Prize De Finibus Terrae - IV edition in memory of Maria Monteduro (Italy). He has been awarded an honorary doctorate "DOCTOR OF LITERATURE" (DOCTOR HONORIS CAUSA) from THE INSTITUTE OF THE EUROPEAN ROMA STUDIES AND RESEARCH INTO CRIME AGAINST HUMANITY AND INTERNATIONAL LAW – BELGRADE (THE REPUBLIC OF SERBIA) and from "BRAZIL INTERNATIONAL COUNCIL CONIPA AND ITMUT INSTITUTE". He has received Uttar Pradesh Gaurav Samman 2019. Presently he acts as III° "SECRETARY-GENERAL OF THE WORLD UNION OF POETS" OF THE HISTORY OF THE WORLD UNION OF POETS FOR THE YEAR 2021. He is the author of 8 books and he is an assistant professor at Eklvaya P. G. College, Banda (U. P.) and he resides at Banda (U. P.) India. Visit him as Dr. Brajesh, email him at dr. mewadevrain@gmail. com, and www. mewadev. com.

SK. Yakubpasha

SK. Yakubpasha working as PGT (English) in TS Model school Karepalli. He contributed his poems "My Childhood Days" "Nature's Trick" "A Silent Song of Tree" and "Mother's Love" to different anthologies of poems. Other poems "Talk of My Shadow" "Mysterious Lady" and "Delight of Nature" published in English Literary Magazines.

Krishnasankar Acharjee

Krishnasankar Acharjee successful English teacher (India-Calcutta-Bengal) is an international free lance writer, poet with several Global Awards. He has been selected as the member of World Union of Poets in Italy, World Icon of Peace and Ambassador in Spain (ROMA -JOTABE), World Laureate in English literature from World Parliament. He has attended National and International Seminar over poetry in different places of the Globe and many of his poems have been published in Journals and Anthologies. He has been acknowledged with the prestigious International Award winning poet in the World.

Binay Laha

Binay Laha is an Indian English poet and editor of *Indology Magazine*. He has authored few books in his credit. He received many awards and felicitations from different national and international organizations for creating and promoting literature. He has been associated with Act local think global, an aesthetic movement to bring the world closer to everybody despite of different history and geography and merit. He is presently associated with **Paschim Bango English Academy** as Secretary General.

Dr. Ratan Ghosh, PhD,

Dr. Ratan Ghosh, PhD, the Associate Editor of an International Literary Journal entitled "THE MIRROR OF TIME" ISSN-2320-012X, free lance writer, poet, and Short Story writer. He has experience of more than 15 years in the field of teaching and research. His poems have been featured in many national and international E- journals, Journals and paper back anthologies across the globe. He has published an anthology of love poems entitled **MY LOVE** and a short story book entitled **THE TALISMAN AND OTHER TALES**. His edited books are **GENDER DISPARITY, NOSTALGIA, CASCADE, SUNUP** and **THE CONTEMPORARY WORLD ENGLISH POETRY.** He has been declared as the **WORLD YOUTH ICON OF LITERATURE,** from **THE NATIONAL ACADEMY OF ARTS AND CULTURE, India affiliated to THE WORLD ACADEMY OF LITERATURE, HISTORY, ARTS AND CULTURE, MEXICO** on 15-11-2019. He has also received "**MEWADEV LAUREL AWARD**" in 2019 from CONTEMPORARY LITERARY SOCIETY OF ALMOR: BANDA (U. P, INDIA) and YOUNG INDOLOGY AWARD, 2020 from INDOLOGY, an international Literary Journal.

CPSIA information can be obtained
at www.ICGtesting.com
Printed in the USA
BVHW040309070623
665472BV00001B/133

9 789390 850488